WADING BIRDS
of the World

WADING BIRDS
of the World

ERIC and **RICHARD SOOTHILL**

BLANDFORD

Blandford Press
An imprint of Cassell
Artillery House, Artillery Row
London SW1P 1RT

Original edition first published 1982
This edition first published in the UK 1989

ISBN 0-7137-2130-8

British Library Cataloguing in Publication Data

Soothill, Eric
  Wading birds of the world.
  1. Charadriiformes
  I. Title II.Soothill, Richard
  598'.33   QL696.C4

Typeset in 9/10 pt Monophoto Baskerville
by Asco Trade Typesetting Ltd, Hong Kong
Printed by Papirografika, Yugoslavia

Dedication

To Gwyneth and Julie

Ruffs and Reeves

Contents

Order—Ciconiiformes

Pseudibis papillosa	Black Ibis	
Geronticus eremita	Bald Ibis	
Nipponia nippon	Japanese Crested Ibis	
Bostrychia carunculata	Wattled Ibis	
Bostrychia hagedash	Hadada Ibis	
Bostrychia olivacea	Olive Ibis	
Bostrychia rara	Spot-breasted Ibis	
Harpiprion caerulescens	Plumbeous Ibis	
Theristicus caudatus	Buff-necked Ibis	
Mesembrinibis cayennensis	Green Ibis	
Phimosus infuscatus	Bare-faced Ibis	
Eudocimus albus	White Ibis	
Eudocimus ruber	Scarlet Ibis	
Cercibis oxycerca	Sharp-tailed Ibis	
Plegadis falcinellus	Glossy Ibis	
Plegadis ridgwayi	Puna Ibis	
Lophotibis cristata	Crested Wood Ibis	
Platalea ajaja	Roseate Spoonbill	
Platalea alba	African Spoonbill	
Platalea flavipes	Yellow-billed Spoonbill	
Platalea leucorodia	White Spoonbill	
Platalea regia	Royal Spoonbill	
Platalea minor	Black-faced Spoonbill	

PHOENICOPTERIDAE	Flamingos	115
Phoeniconaias minor	Lesser Flamingo	
Phoenicopterus chilensis	Chilean Flamingo	
Phoenicoparrus andinus	Andean Flamingo	
Phoenicoparrus jamesi	James' Flamingo	
Phoenicopterus ruber	Greater Flamingo	

Order—Gruiformes

GRUIDAE	Cranes	120
Grus antigone	Sarus Crane	
Grus americana	Whooping Crane	
Grus canadensis	Sandhill Crane	
Grus carunculatus	Wattled Crane	
Grus grus	Common Crane	
Grus japonensis	Japanese Crane	
Grus leucogeranus	Siberian White Crane	
Grus monacha	Hooded Crane	
Grus nigricollis	Black-necked Crane	
Grus rubicunda	Brolga	
Grus vipio	White-naped Crane	
Anthropoides paradisea	Blue Crane	
Anthropoides virgo	Demoiselle Crane	
Balearica pavonina	Crowned Crane	

ARAMIDAE	Limpkin	136
Aramus guarauna	Limpkin	

Charadrius alticola	Puna Plover
Charadrius asiaticus	Caspian Sand Plover
Charadrius bicinctus	Banded Dotterel
Charadrius cinctus	Red-kneed Dotterel
Charadrius collaris	Collared Plover
Charadrius cucullatus	Hooded Dotterel
Charadrius dubius	Little Ringed Plover
Charadrius falklandicus	Two-banded Plover
Charadrius forbesi	Forbes's Banded Plover
Charadrius hiaticula	Ringed Plover
Charadrius leschenaultii	Greater Sand Plover
Charadrius marginatus	White-fronted Sand Plover
Charadrius melanops	Black-fronted Plover
Charadrius melodus	Piping Plover
Charadrius mongolus	Mongolian Plover
Charadrius montana	Mountain Plover
Charadrius novaeseelandiae	New Zealand Shore Plover
Charadrius obscurus	Red breasted Dotterel
Charadrius pecuarius	Kittlitz's Sand Plover
Charadrius peroni	Malay Plover
Charadrius placidus	Long-billed Ringed Plover
Charadrius semipalmatus	Semipalmated Plover
Charadrius thoracicus	Black-banded Sand Plover
Charadrius tricollaris	Three-banded Plover
Charadrius venustus	Chestnut-banded Sand Plover
Charadrius veredus	Oriental Plover
Charadrius vociferus	Killdeer
Charadrius wilsonia	Wilson's Plover
Oreopholus ruficollis	Tawny-throated Dotterel
Zonibyx modestus	Rufous-chested Dotterel
Anarhynchus frontalis	Wrybill
Pluvianellus socialis	Magellanic Plover
Eudromias morinellus	Dotterel
Phegornis mitchellii	Diademed Sandpiper Plover

Bartramia longicauda	Upland Sandpiper
Numenius americanus	Long-billed Curlew
Numenius arquata	Eurasian Curlew
Numenius borealis	Eskimo Curlew
Numenius minutus	Little Curlew
Numenius phaeopus	Whimbrel
Numenius tahitiensis	Bristle-thighed Curlew
Numenius tenuirostris	Slender-billed Curlew
Limosa fedoa	Marbled Godwit
Limosa haemastica	Hudsonian Godwit
Limosa lapponica	Bar-tailed Godwit
Limosa limosa	Black-tailed Godwit
Tringa brevipes	Grey-tailed Tattler
Tringa cancellatus	Tuamotu Sandpiper
Tringa cinereus	Terek Sandpiper

Tringa erythropus	Spotted Redshank
Tringa flavipes	Lesser Yellowlegs
Tringa glareola	Wood Sandpiper
Tringa guttifer	Spotted Greenshank
Tringa hypoleucos	Common Sandpiper
Tringa incana	Wandering Tattler
Tringa macularia	Spotted Sandpiper
Tringa melanoleuca	Greater Yellowlegs
Tringa nebularia	Greenshank
Tringa ochropus	Green Sandpiper
Tringa solitaria	Solitary Sandpiper
Tringa stagnatilis	Marsh Sandpiper
Tringa totanus	Common Redshank
Catoptrophorus semipalmatus	Willet
Gallinago andina	Puna Snipe
Gallinago gallinago	Common Snipe
Gallinago hardwickii	Japanese Snipe
Gallinago imperialis	Banded Snipe
Gallinago jamesoni	Andean Snipe
Gallinago macrodactyla	Madagascar Snipe
Gallinago media	Great Snipe
Gallinago megala	Swinhoe's Snipe
Gallinago nemoricola	Wood Snipe
Gallinago nigripennis	African Snipe
Gallinago nobilis	Noble Snipe
Gallinago paraguayiae	Paraguayan Snipe
Gallinago solitaria	Solitary Snipe
Gallinago stenura	Pintail Snipe
Gallinago stricklandii	Cordilleran Snipe
Gallinago undulata	Giant Snipe
Arenaria interpres	Turnstone
Arenaria melanocephala	Black Turnstone
Limnodromus griseus	Short-billed Dowitcher
Limnodromus scolopaceus	Long-billed Dowitcher
Limnodromus semipalmatus	Asian Dowitcher
Coenocorypha pusilla	Chatham Island Snipe
Coenocorypha aucklandica	New Zealand Snipe
Scolopax celebensis	Celebes Woodcock
Scolopax minor	American Woodcock
Scolopax mira	Amami Woodcock
Scolopax rochussenii	Obi Woodcock
Scolopax rusticola	Eurasian Woodcock
Scolopax saturata	East Indian Woodcock
Lymnocryptes minimus	Jack Snipe
Aphriza virgata	Surfbird
Calidris acuminata	Sharp-tailed Sandpiper
Calidris alba	Sanderling
Calidris alpinus	Dunlin
Calidris bairdii	Baird's Sandpiper
Calidris canutus	Knot
Calidris ferruginea	Curlew Sandpiper

Acknowledgements

We should like to express our thanks to the following people who, during the past few years, have given freely of their help in so many ways:

Australia
Vincent Serventy

Canada
Jim and Elaine Doke, Fawcet
Randy Evans, Alberta Game Farm, near Edmonton
Edgar T. Jones
Gary R. Jones who sadly died in a fire in 1980
Doug Kauffman, Tofield
M.R. Robertson (Regional Director) and
Alan R. Smith of the Canadian Wildlife Service, Edmonton
Stan and Shirley Viste, Hanna
Maxwell W. Ward (President) of Wardair Canada

Denmark
Ricard Nielsen

Finland
Mikko Ojanen
Nils Fritzēn

France
Michel Czajkowski

Great Britain
Ron Barker
Ian C.J. Galbraith, British Museum (Natural History)
Dennis Johnson
John and Anne-Marie Larman
Catherine Pollock
Roy Scholes
Rochdale Lending Library (The staff)
Ralph Walker
Peter Whitehead
Andy Wooldridge
Gordon Yeates

Holland
Harry Fabritius

Sweden
Sam and Irja Ehrlin
Sören Svensson

USA
Barbara Linton, Associate Librarian, National Audubon Society
Dr Ernie Wells, for his help and companionship in Alberta during the spring of 1979

Introduction

As the term 'wading birds' is often confused with 'waders' and 'shorebirds' it is as well to explain what we mean by the term in the context of this book. It is generally accepted that the sub-order Charadrii comprises the 'waders' of Europe, or 'shore-birds' of North America. However, 'wading birds' here are taken to include all those birds which actually do wade at some time of the year, especially in their search for food; whether in deep water, at the water's edge, along the tide-line or in other areas of wetland. Therefore we also include several families from the orders Ciconiiformes and Gruiformes along with those of the order Charadriiformes.

Those birds that are not included, but which might be thought to qualify for inclusion deserve some mention. The Jacanas or Lily-trotters (Jacanidae) are not included as they do not, strictly speaking, wade. They are long-legged birds whose lives seem mostly spent walking about on the leaves of water-lilies and other aquatic vegetation, this being possible by virtue of their very long toes and long straight claws. Food items are picked from the water by their slender plover-like bills. The Coursers and Pratincoles (Glareolidae) are also omitted with the exception of *Pluvianus aegyptius*, the Egyptian Plover, and *Peltohyas australis*, the Australian dotterel, which we accord the benefit of the doubt! Coursers are specially adapted for a life in desert conditions: their pointed and slightly downward-curved bill seems well designed for catching or picking-up insects. They are very fast runners and do not probe the ground or wade in search of food. Pratincoles frequent areas of flat, open, and often quite infertile land; especially those regions adjacent to river deltas, the shores of lakes and lagoons, and other areas that are periodically subjected to flooding. The diet consists of insects such as dragonflies, caddisflies, beetles, gnats and the like, most of which are caught on the wing. Pratincoles may often be seen hawking their prey; wading is not involved. The Seed Snipes (Thinocoridae) are restricted to South America, mainly Ecuador, Peru, western Bolivia, Chile, western Argentina, southern Patagonia, and Tierra del Fuego. These short-legged birds, with somewhat partridge-like proportions and posture, have short stocky finch-like bills and, as their name suggests, are seed-eaters. Sheath-bills (Chionididae) breed exclusively in coastal regions of the

Antarctic and sub-Antarctic; there are but two species, *Chionis alba*, Yellow-billed Sheath-bill and *C. minor* the Black-billed Sheath-bill. They acquire food chiefly by scavenging, but also eat algae which they scrape off intertidal rocks, and should a dead fish or squid be washed ashore these too will occasionally be included in their diet. Sheath-bills are thought to be the link that connects the waders and the gulls.

The Phalaropes (Phalaropididae) we do include, even though all three species have feet which are particularly well adapted for swimming, and indeed much of their food is picked from the water surface whilst doing just that. The Grey Phalarope, *Phalaropus fulicarius*, spends much of its life in close association with the sea; of the three species, Wilson's Phalarope, *P. tricolor*, wades in search of food more frequently than either *P. fulicarius* or *P. lobatus*. It is interesting to look at the natural factors which have always governed competition between related species as they search for food: chiefly, in this group, these factors are quite simply length and design of bill, and length of leg. If we watch the Spotted Redshank feeding in company with the Common Redshank, we notice that the former by virtue of its longer legs can feed wading in depths that would present difficulties to the latter. The point becomes much more exaggerated when we consider the long legs of the godwits and compare them with the short legs of both Sanderling and Dunlin. The long bills of the godwits and the curlews enable them to probe deep into the mud and so they collect food items at different depths from the shorter-billed species. Plovers, for example, having relatively short bills, are able to probe only a little way below the surface. Catching methods vary, too, depending on different capabilities: flamingos sift the water for food whereas the herons step quietly and warily as they search for fish; the taller species are well able to stalk in waters beyond the reach of their shorter-legged cousins and are often seeking quite different prey.

In contrast to the pleasingly ordered and relatively predictable world of natural competition it is a cause for worldwide concern that, in the face of competition from man, wading birds are suffering, in particular, a serious decline in the number of suitable feeding grounds and breeding sites. Feeding areas are disappearing as marshlands and other wetlands are reclaimed for agriculture, industry and other commercial uses. Building projects may encroach too closely on a favourite feeding or breeding ground. In some areas trees may be felled adjacent to those which for generations have been the ancestral homes of herons or other tree-nesting species; the disturbance caused is often sufficient for the birds to desert and seek out alternative sites.

Another hazard is that of pollution, which affects all wildlife dependent on the sea: wading birds are not so vulnerable to oil spillage at sea as, say, members of the auk family, but the insidious pollution of tide-lines around the world takes it toll, and although preservation of wetland habitat is recognised as a priority issue in conservation, the battle will remain an uphill one for many years to come.

Family—Ardeidae

Herons, Bitterns
(61 species recorded)

Grey Heron
(European Grey Heron)

Ardea cinerea

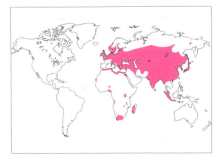

Description Length, including neck and legs, 98 cm. Standing 75 cm. Male mainly ashy grey above; crown white with long black crest on nape. The black line through eye extends to the crest. Neck white with a dotted black line running centrally down front. The long white feathers of the breast streaked with black. Tail and wings grey, the latter with black flight feathers. Remaining underparts greyish-white. Iris golden yellow. Bill long and pointed, yellowish when breeding, but dark horny brown at other times. Legs and feet yellowish in breeding birds, occasionally tinged with pink; at other times greenish-brown with yellow marks on joints and rear of tarsi. Female very similar but smaller, with less well developed occipital crest and pectoral plumes. The Eastern Grey Heron (*A.c. rectirostris*) is very similar but paler grey above, and not recognised universally as a subspecies.

Characteristics and Behaviour

The large size is sufficient to distinguish it from other European herons. Flight distinctive, with neck pulled into shoulders and S-shaped, the legs trailing out behind. Progresses with steady and deliberate flaps of its broad, rounded wings. Gregarious when nesting, outside breeding season usually a solitary bird, but may be encounteed in small groups.

Habitat A very wide ranging habitat, showing preference for low-lying areas with rivers, lakes and ponds; also salt marshes, brackish lagoons and coastal areas. In fact can be met with in most watery situations that are not polluted.

Food Consists of fish, frogs, molluscs, aquatic insects and crustaceans; also small rodents, young birds and, surprisingly, even water rails have been recorded. Hunts mainly during the hours of dusk and dawn, either by standing motionless at the water's edge or by wading in the shallows. The long pointed bill shoots out with amazing speed and the prey is caught between the mandibles. Fish are always swallowed head first and are skilfully manoeuvred into this position.

Voice When in flight or if disturbed, a harsh 'frarnk' or 'quaarnk'. Also produces a variety of guttural noises and 'honks' in the nesting vicinity.

Display Various postures with neck held in upright or horizontal positions, and plumes raised. Also dancing display during courtship. Bill snapping can be heard from nesting birds.

Breeding Nests are constructed during February and eggs laid in March, if the weather is not severely cold. A social nester usually in mixed colonies with other species (not mixed in Britain). A platform of twigs is constructed in a tree or shrub (usually standing in or close to water), which becomes quite large after several years' occupation. Eggs usually three to four and in some shade of pale greeny blue. Size 58.5 × 43.5 mm. Incubation begins with first egg and is shared by both sexes for a period of 25–26 days. Nest building and feeding of young (by regurgitation) are also shared.

18

Grey Heron (*Ardea cinerea*)

A.c. rectirostris differs only in breeding season, this being March to June in Kashmir; July to October in northern India; and November to March in southern India and Sri Lanka.

Distribution Breeds in the Palearctic and Ethiopian regions. In Europe, breeds in Great Britain, Finland, Sweden, Denmark, East and West Germany, Switzerland, Belgium, the Netherlands and France. Also along the North African coast, parts of South Africa, Asia Minor to north-western Siberia. *A.c. rectirostris* breeds throughout India and Pakistan, Bangladesh, Nepal and Sri Lanka, the Maldive, Andaman and Nicobar Islands. Also the Middle East, Burma and Thailand. *A.c. monicae* breeds on the islands of Banc d'Arguin. *A.c. jouyi* breeds in Japan, China, Malaya, Indochina, Sumatra and Java. *A.c. firasa* breeds in Madagascar. *A.c. altirostris* breeds in Java and Sumatra.

Cocoi Heron

Ardea cocoi

Description Length 97–127 cm, being larger at the southern end of its range. Crown, face (to below eye), nape and nuchal crest black. Chin, throat and neck white, with central foreneck boldly streaked black, and long hackles of lower neck overhanging upper breast. Rest of upperparts pale grey, shading to whitish on wing coverts and tips of elongated scapulars. Black patch on shoulder of wing; flight feathers blackish. Underparts white with large black patches on either side of lower breast and abdomen. Bare facial skin blue. Iris yellow. Bill dull yellow, paling towards tip and pinkish towards base (when breeding). Legs and feet blackish-brown. Sexes alike.

Habitat and Distribution Frequents the shores of lakes, swamps and rivers (but not in dense forest). Nests in reed beds, bushes and in trees, usually over water. Season July in Surinam; October in Uruguay; and November in Buenos Aires. Breeds in South America from Panama south to Aisén in Chile and Chubut in Argentina. Visits Trinidad as a non-breeder, usually between January and June.

Goliath Heron
(Giant Heron)

Ardea goliath

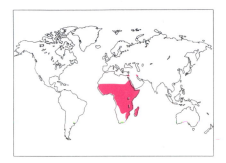

Description Length about 156 cm. Crown and crest, sides and back of neck in shades of chestnut. Upperparts, wings and tail grey, a few feathers tipped with white. Cheeks, chin and throat white. Foreneck white, boldly streaked with black. Lower parts including underwing deep dull chestnut. Lores greenish-yellow. Iris yellow, outer rim red when breeding. Bill long and pointed, black above, lower mandible much paler, tending towards yellow. Legs and feet dark greyish-black. Sexes alike.

Characteristics and Behaviour A solitary and very shy bird, difficult to approach. Its enormous size prevents confusion with the Purple Heron (*A. purpurea*), being much more heavily proportioned, especially about the neck. If disturbed it is quick to rise on those broad, rounded wings, uttering a deep grating 'kraak kraak'. Has a very slow but methodical wing beat and flies with neck pulled well into shoulders and legs extended behind.

Habitat Frequents inland lakes with dense marginal vegetation, papyrus swamps, estuaries, mangrove swamps and tidal creeks. Not often encountered on dry land.

Food Feeds almost entirely on fish, which it catches in a manner typical of the genus. Because of its large size, it can wade to greater depths of water than other herons and so there should be no real competition for food. Even so, it is regularly mobbed and harassed by other species of heron, although one Goliath is quite capable of staving off an assault mounted by several other birds. Mullet, eels, barbel, carp and catfish are included in the diet, individual fish often weighing several pounds.

Voice Thought to be very much a silent bird, the only call on record being a deep harsh 'kraak kraak' when disturbed.

Display The courtship ritual is not known, but is probably as for other members of the genus.

Breeding Not a colonial nester, possibly because is not abundant anywhere, although it sometimes nests within the bounds of a colony of other heron species. Breeding occurs September to December in South Africa; early autumn in other parts of southern Africa. In the northern tropics breeds either spring or autumn. A platform of sticks and reeds about 1 m in diameter is built on flattened sedge or papyrus, or perhaps in a partly submerged bush, always close to water and usually about 1 m above it. The two to four eggs are chalky blue and measure 73 × 53 mm, which seems surprisingly small for so large a bird. Incubation continues for about four weeks and the nestling period is about five or six weeks.

Distribution Occurs from Senegal and the northern Sudan to parts of South Africa, also Madagascar. Recorded from Natal and Transvaal, but rarely on the east coast. Breeds in Botswana and around the Okavango River in northern Namibia. Outside Africa the only definite breeding area is in Iraq. Mainly resident within Africa but a rare vagrant in Pakistan and India.

Goliath Heron (*Ardea goliath*)

Great Blue Heron

Ardea herodias

Description Length variable, 97–137 cm. Forehead and most of crown white, margined with black; this black extends backwards from over the eyes terminating in two 23-cm-long occipital plumes. Rest of head white, except for a small area of bluey-black plumage near base of bill. Sides and back of neck tinged with pinkish-grey, front of neck whitish and longitudinally streaked with black. Long plumes emanate at base of neck to fall loosely over upper breast. Rest of upperparts bluish-grey offset by a prominent black shoulder patch with a smaller patch of cinnamon immediately to the rear which is sometimes concealed by folded wing. Sides and flanks bluish-slate; breast and belly black with broad white streaks; thighs dull orangey yellow. Nuptial reddening of the yellow iris occurs, the normally yellowish bill turns orangey red except for brown culmen and tip, the dark greenish-brown legs flush pink or scarlet, and the dull green loral skin becomes a brilliant lime green. These bright colours fade soon after eggs have been laid. Sexes alike. The various subspecies mainly differ from each other in the darkness of the neck and upperparts and, more importantly, in size. However, any given figure for average lengths is misleading, since the females may be up to 10% smaller than the males. The American Great White Heron (*A.h. occidentalis*) is a subspecies of predominantly white plumage, with tibia yellowish, shading downward to slate grey; tarsus slate grey.

Characteristics and Behaviour Distinguishable from both the Grey Heron (*A. cinerea*) and the Cocoi Heron (*A. cocoi*), by its tinge of pinkish-grey on neck and cinnamon on thighs. The Cocoi Heron also differs in having an all black crown. Generally wary and very cautious. Flies with slow and dignified strokes of the wings, with folded neck and extended legs.

Habitat Frequents a great variety of freshwater wetlands including streams, rivers, lakes, ponds and swamps, but seems equally tolerant of salt water areas. Can be found up to altitudes of 1500 m in Panama.

Food Its hunting techniques are similar to those of the Grey Heron, and include standing and patiently waiting, slow stalking, and very occasionally diving. The diet consists of fish, amphibians, small mammals (both aquatic and terrestrial), crustaceans, reptiles, birds and insects, with occasional vegetable matter. Pilfering of food from domestic animals, and (rarely) killing fowl, are also recorded.

Voice Generally a silent bird giving utterance to the occasional gruff croaking 'grak'.

Display The onset of the breeding season is greeted by so-called dancing displays, although their importance or significance is open to doubt. They involve several birds strutting and jumping into the air in an adopted upright posture. On deciding nesting sites, territorial displays and courtship seem to be identical to those of the Grey Heron.

Breeding Tall trees, bushes (Dowling Lake, Hanna, Alberta), rocks, cliff ledges and even the ground (particularly in reeds and rushes), all provide suitable nesting sites. They breed colonially either with their own kind or mixed with other herons, cormorants, pelicans or spoonbills. The nest is a large structure of sticks and twigs collected by the male but assembled by the female. The clutch varies between three to seven eggs, tending to increase with latitude. The eggs are pale bluish-green or olive, the average size of those of the small nominate race being 65 × 46 mm. These are amongst the largest and are only slightly smaller than those of the largest subspecies. In southern localities breeding grounds are occupied by early February, but although laying in the north sometimes occurs before the end of March it is usually not until late April. Incubation continues for about 28 days and is shared by both birds.

Distribution The overlapping boundaries of the subspecies make knowledge of their breeding range rather patchy. The nominate's range extends from Nova Scotia westwards to Alberta with its most northerly point near Edmonton at about 55°N. From here it stretches to the south-east corner of British Columbia. In the USA it breeds from Maine and the Atlantic seaboard south to South Carolina, west through the northern states to the Rockies and beyond to north-east Washington. Along the Pacific coast it is replaced by two subspecies: *A.h. fannini* from Cape Disappointment north to the Alaskan peninsula at almost 60°N, and *A.h. hyperonca* from Oregon through California to just beyond the Mexican border. Inland along the Sierra Nevada, *A.h. treganzai* replaces *A.h. hyperonca* with its range covering the majority of the western and south-western States down to the Gulf Coast in Texas. Here *A.h. wardi* takes its place, breeding from Kansas and Oklahoma across the Mississippi basin to Georgia, south to Florida and along the rest of the Gulf coast. *A.h. sanctilucae* occurs on Espiritu Santo, off Baja California in Mexico. *A.h. cognata* occurs on the Galapagos Islands. *A.h. occidentalis* has a greatly res-

Great Blue Heron (*Ardea herodias*)

tricted range, breeding only in the extreme south of Florida and on some of the Florida Keys. Also occurs in Cuba and Jamaica. The nominate's post-breeding dispersal extends to Newfoundland and Greenland, whilst its migration takes it as far as Panama. In winter *A.h. wardi* and *A.h. treganzai* become common in Florida and Texas, also reaching Mexico, where *A.h. hyperonca* has also been seen. The other four subspecies are subject only to local movements.

Malagasy Heron
(Madagascar Heron)

Ardea humbloti

Description Length 95 cm. Crown, nuchal crest, foreface and chin black. Wings and tail dusky grey. Rest of plumage dull fawny grey, much darker altogether than the Grey Heron (*A. cinerea*). Iris yellow. Bill long, heavy, dull yellow, dusky at base. Legs and feet dull brown. Sexes alike.

Habitat and Distribution Frequents both saltwater and freshwater areas. Few nesting records available, but is known to nest on ground as well as in trees. Perhaps most common in western Madagascar; also seen regularly around Lake Alaotra. Was once thought to be restricted to Madagascar but has recently been seen on Moheli and Mayotte in the Comoros.

Great White-bellied Heron

Ardea imperialis

Description Length 127 cm. Crown, face and upperneck pale fawny grey. Chin and throat white. Neck and upper breast grey with long hackles. Back, wings and tail browny grey. Thigh coverts greyish. Rest of underparts white. Loral and orbital skin, and base of lower mandible yellowish-green. Iris yellow. Bill, upper mandible and inner edge of lower mandible dusky grey; tip and underparts of lower mandible greenish-yellow, remainder of lower mandible dark grey. Legs and feet blackish. Sexes alike.

Habitat and Distribution Not a coastal species, favours forest rivers and inland swamps. The nest is an immense platform of sticks in the uppermost part of a tall tree. Resident but rare in Nepal and Sikkim, Bihar (north of the Ganges

River), Bhutan to north-eastern Assam and Bangladesh. Also found in Burma where the upper reaches of the Irrawaddy River are regarded as one of the bird's strongholds. Only breeding record comes from Arakan (Burma) during April.

Great white-bellied Heron

Black-headed Heron
Ardea melanocephala

Description Length 92 cm. Forehead, crown, nape, crest and back of neck entirely black. Chin and lower throat white; upper foreneck stippled black and white. Rest of plumage mainly grey. Lores yellowish-green. Iris yellow, becoming red when breeding. Bill, upper mandible blackish, lower greenish-yellow. Legs black. Sexes alike. On rare occasions a melanistic form occurs, in which the chin and entire upperparts are black.

Habitat and Distribution Equally at home on dry or wet land, but does require water somewhere within vicinity. The nest, which is occupied at all times of the year with occasionally two or even three broods being reared, consists of a platform of twigs constructed high in the top of a tree. Confined to Africa south of the Sahara, its breeding range extends from Senegal in the west to the Sudan, and south to Cape Province. However, within this range its distribution is fragmentary, for instance in South Africa nesting has only been recorded in the Transvaal apart from Cape Province.

White-faced Heron
Ardea novaehollandiae

Description Length 60 cm with neck extended. Forehead, face and throat white. Crown, nape, neck, wings, back and tail in shades of medium to dark grey. Main flight feathers black. Long hackles along edges of back and lower neck (the latter tinged russet). Breast, belly and undershoulders pale grey. Facial skin blue-grey. Iris yellow. Bill black, pale grey at base of lower mandible. Legs dull yellow. Sexes alike. The subspecies *A.n. parry* has a darker plumage overall.

Habitat and Distribution Crepuscular to nocturnal in habit. Frequents both coastal and inland swamps in the vicinity of wooded areas. Nests chiefly July to April, a platform of twigs being constructed in a tree fork or on a branch, at heights between 7 and 20 m. Fairly common throughout Australia and Tasmania, also occurs in New Zealand and New Guinea. *A.n. parry* breeds in the north of Western Australia.

White-necked Heron
Ardea pacifica

Description Length 75 cm with neck extended. Head and neck white, with black spots down centre of foreneck. Long white upper neck hackles and lower dull maroon hackles hang over breast. Wings, back and tail black sheened with dark bluish-green. Long dull maroon hackles along edges of back. Breast and belly brownish-grey, broadly streaked with white centrally. Facial skin greenish-yellow. Iris yellowish. Bill black, yellow at base of lower mandible. Legs and feet black. Sexes alike. Ornamental hackles lacking outside breeding season, and more black spotting on foreneck in winter. White shoulder patch apparent in flight.

Habitat and Distribution Frequents freshwater localities and marshes, seldom on coast. A colonial or solitary nester constructing a platform in a tree close to or over water, at heights of up to 30 m. Confined as a breeding species to Australia, Tasmania and the Bass Strait Islands. Season mainly September to April.

Pied Heron
Ardea picata
(Egretta picata also *Hydranassa picata)*

Description Length 45 cm. Predominantly black with a slaty-blue sheen. Feathers of nape extended to form long blackish plumes. Throat and foreneck white, a few longish white feathers extending over upper breast. Naked facial skin dark greyish-brown. Iris yellow. Bill long, pointed and yellow. Legs greenish-yellow. Sexes alike.

Habitat and Distribution A tree-nesting species in mangroves at heights of about 4–5 m. Eggs laid March/April with most young flying by end of May. Breeds commonly in Australia along northern coast of Northern Territory, north-eastern coastal regions of Western Australia, and both north and eastern coasts of Queensland. The species extends to the Celebes.

Purple Heron

Ardea purpurea

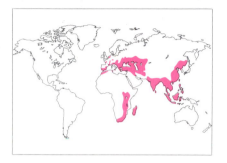

Description Length 79 cm. Sides of face and neck rufous buff, with two black stripes extending from below the eye, one down side of neck, the other down nape. Crown and plumes black. Throat, chin, cheeks and foreneck white and pale buff, the latter boldly streaked with black. Elongated whitish feathers hang from lower neck and chest. Mantle and wing coverts slate grey; scapulars elongated and pale greyish chestnut when breeding. Rump and tail grey. Belly, breast and shoulders of wings vinaceous chestnut, darkest on belly; flanks brownish-grey; undertail coverts blackish. Bill bright buffish-yellow (when breeding), long, slender and pointed. Naked skin of lores yellowish-green. Iris yellow. Legs blackish-brown in front, sullied buff behind; feet dark brown above, dusky buff beneath; toes long. Sexes alike.

Characteristics and Behaviour Smaller and more slightly built than the Grey Heron (*A. cinerea*). In flight, the neck is pulled into the shoulder producing a noticeable bulge. The wings are also narrower than those of the Grey. A solitary bird, very wary, and seldom seen away from the dense cover of its habitat.

Habitat Inhabits dense reed beds in swampy areas such as ditches, the margins of lakes and river banks. The subspecies *A.p. bournei* frequents tall mangrove trees in deeply ravined areas.

Food Stalks very slowly in shallow water, stopping occasionally to strike out at its prey. Principally takes fish and aquatic insects, also amphibians, small mammals, crustaceans, molluscs, spiders, lizards and snakes. Usually feeds during the late evening and early morning.

Voice The most vocal period is when breeding, a wide variety of harsh calls issue from the nesting colonies. The flight calls 'frarnk' or 'krreck' are very like those of the Grey Heron, but not so loud and pitched a little higher.

Display Stretches upwards to the full extent of body, neck and legs, with bill pointing skywards and feathers of neck erected. Then goes into an almost reversed posture, crouched on bended legs with head retracted. Bill clapping is performed throughout these displays. Body swaying and head bobbing are also practised.

Breeding In central Europe eggs are laid from April to June; in southern Europe breeding commences a little earlier. Usually a colonial nester, a pile of dead reed stems being constructed in a dense reed bed, at a height of 0.5–1 m and not too far from open water. Occasionally built of small branches and twigs in a tree at heights of up to 25 m. Usual clutch size is two to five pale blue-green eggs which often become stained during incubation. They are laid at intervals of two or three days and measure 57 × 41 mm. Incubation continues for 26 days and commences with the first egg, both sexes taking part.

Distribution Breeds in south-west Palearctic region, eastwards to Turkestan and Iran, also East and South Africa. Most of the birds breeding in west Palearctic winter south of the Sahara. *A.p. bournei* breeds and is resident on Santiago, Cape Verde Islands. *A.p. madagascariensis* breeds Madagascar

Purple Heron (*Ardea purpurea*)

and is both a resident and local migrant. *A.p. manilensis* breeds throughout the plains of India east to Assam and Manipur, Pakistan, Nepal, Bangladesh, Sri Lanka, the Andaman Islands, Burma, Thailand, Indochina, China (south of the Yangtze), the Ryukyu Islands and south to the Philippines, Sumatra, Java and the Celebes.

Sumatran Heron
(Dusky-grey Heron)

Ardea sumatrana

Description Length 115 cm, smallest of the three giant herons. General coloration brownish-grey, darkest on wings and back, and with a slight pinkish tinge on face and neck. When breeding has greyish-white tipped plumes on nape, scapulars and upper breast. Loral and orbital skin pale sullied green or yellowish-green. Iris yellow. Bill mainly black, but yellowish at base and beneath lower mandible. Legs dusky brown. Sexes alike. *A.s. mathewsi* has an almost bronzy tinge and a longer bill.

Habitat and Distribution Frequents coastal mangroves and creeks, and occasionally dense forest-fringed channels inland. The platform nests are built on horizontal branches often overhanging water. Breeding season May and June. Widespread in Malaya, also breeds on south-west and south-east coasts of Thailand, the western Arakan coast of Burma, south Vietnam, the Philippines, the Celebes and Borneo; a few records from the Sunda Islands (where it was first discovered in Sumatra). *A.s. mathewsi* (nests recorded in July, November, February and April) inhabits the coastlands of northern Australia from Derby in the west to Rockhampton in the east, perhaps also reaching New South Wales.

Green-backed Heron
(Striated Heron or Little Green Heron)

Butorides striatus

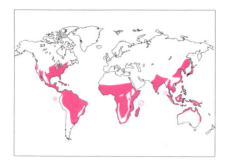

Description   Length 46 cm. Forehead, crown and long crest glossy greenish-black. Head and neck grey. Cheeks, chin and centre of breast white. The grey upperparts have glossy sheens of dark green, and green tinged with bronze. Wing coverts shiny dark green, green wing quills glossed black, the tips and margins edged with grey and white. Underparts ashy grey; white under tail coverts tipped and edged with black. Eyelids and bare patch in front of eyes yellowish leaf green. Iris lemon yellow. Bill, upper mandible dark brown, lower sage green, somewhat blacker in breeding condition. Legs and feet yellowish leaf green. Sexes alike. There are many subspecies, some of which differ slightly in plumage and/or size: the Darker Maldivian Green Heron (*B.s. albidulus*) is paler than the nominate; the Paler Maldivian Green Heron (*B.s. didii*) is even paler; the Andaman Little Green Heron (*B.s. spodiogaster*) is darker than the nominate; *B.s. virescens* is darker greenish-grey with reddish-brown on neck; the Lava Heron (*B.s. sundevallii*) is much darker overall grey.

Characteristics and Behaviour   A shy, silent and retiring bird, solitary in its habits. Smaller than the Pond Heron, appearing mainly black, grey and dark glossy green. Chiefly nocturnal or cre-puscular but can be more active during daytime if cloudy or overcast when it may be encountered in some shady spot at rest, perched on a tree branch or projecting root just a foot or so above the water, with tail constantly flicking. When taken by surprise will flush on slow but deliberate flapping wings with neck held outstretched; a heavy looking bird when in flight.

Habitat   Fond of shady situations along watercourses or jungle streams especially in rock pools; also lakes and ponds with dense shrubby marginal growth. Frequents plains and peninsular hills up to 1000 m. Also met with in mangrove swamps, quiet coastal back-waters and tidal inlets.

Food   Will either seek food by walking stealthily along the water's edge, ready to strike out with the bill should suitable prey be within reach; or will stand patiently, with outdrawn neck waiting to lunge at edible items that swim or float by. The diet includes crabs, shrimps, water beetles, frogs and mudfish.

Voice   Except when flushed usually a silent bird, the alarm notes are 'k'yow-k'yow' or 'k'yek-k'yek', also 'tewn-tewn-twen'.

Display   Constant raising of crest feathers, up and down flicking of tail; also has a 'flap flight display'. Duets between male and female described as 'skow-skeowbouts'.

Breeding   The nest is usually built in a small tree in a mangrove swamp, or maybe in the concealment of a bush alongside a stream; at heights of 3–4.5 m. A collection of twigs are arranged into a small platform; the depression remains unlined. Nests singly at all times. The three to five pale glaucous eggs are of smooth texture and measure 39.5 × 29.7 mm. Incubation commences with the first egg and is undertaken by both sexes; period unrecorded. The young are fed by regurgitation, a duty shared by male and female. Over most of Pakistan and India the breeding period extends from March to September; in Sri Lanka from March to July; varying locally with water conditions. It is evidently double brooded.

Distribution The nominate (*B.s. striatus*) breeds only on Isabela Island and Santa Cruz. However, there are many subspecies which give the species as a whole a very widespread distribution. There are 21 Old World and 13 New World subspecies:

OLD WORLD

Asian region: *abbotti*—Malaya; *actophilus* —northern Burma, Indochina and south China coast, migrating south to Malaysia and Indonesia; *albidulus*—southern Maldives; *amurensis*—Amur valleys, north-east China, Korea and Japan, migrating south to south-east China, Taiwan, the Philippines and Sulawesi; *chloriceps*—Sind, Nepal, Assam and rest of India, Burma, Laccadive Islands and Sri Lanka; *connectens*—greater part of China, difficult to differentiate from *actophilus* except by size but appears to be less migratory; *didii*—central and northern Maldives; *javanicus* —Indonesia, suspected to be a resident subspecies of Malaysia and Sri Lanka; *moluccarum*—Buru, Ambon and Seram, south Moluccas; *spodiogaster*—Andamans, Nicobar and West Sumatra, differs from *chloriceps* in being smaller and darker. African region: *albolimbatus*—Diego Garcia, Chagos archipelago; *atricapillus*—tropical Africa from Senegal and the Sudan, to eastern Cape Province; *brevipes*—Red Sea coasts and Somalia; *crawfordii*—Assumption and Aldabra Islands; *degens* —Seychelles; *rhizophorae*—Comoros, resembles *javanicus* of the Asian region; *rutenbergi*—Madagascar and Mascarenes. Australasian and Oceania regions: *macrorhynchus*—New Guinea, Solomons and eastern Australia; *patruelis*—Tahiti and other South Pacific Islands; *rogersi*—mid-west of Australia but of un-

Green-backed Heron (*Butorides striatus atricapillus*)

certain status and quite possibly just an erythristic form of *stagnatilis* from north-west Australia and Northern Territory coastland areas.

NEW WORLD

North and Central America and West Indian regions: *anthonyi*—California, Arizona and north-west Mexico, migrating to west Mexico; *bahamensis*—Bahamas; *curacensis*—Curaçao and Bonaire; *frazari*—southern Baja California; *maculatus*—Antilles and east coast of Central America as far as Panama Canal; *margaritophilus*—Pearl Island in the Bay of Panama; *virescens*—eastern North America from Nova Scotia and southern Ontario, and eastern Mexico, migrating as far as Panama. South American region; *cyanurus*—Paraguay, Uruguay and northern Argentina; *fusicollis*—the Buenos Aires region of central Argentina; *patens*—canal zone of Panama, of uncertain status and quite possibly intermediate between northern and southern populations; *robinsoni*—Margarita Island, Venezuela; *sundevalli*—Galapagos Islands.

Lava Heron

Butorides striatus sundevalli

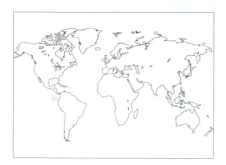

Description   Length 40 cm. The darkest of all the subspecies, with an overall dark grey appearance, although it shares certain characteristics with the majority of the subspecies such as a green erectile crown, green wing coverts and scapulars; though this colour often appears blackish or blue rather than green. At the onset of the breeding season changes occur in the soft-part colours, the dark blue or greenish lores become yellow; the yellow iris turns to deep orange; the dusky yellow bill with its greenish-yellow base becomes glossy black; and the dusky or greenish-yellow legs become bright yellow, orange, or reddish-orange. These colour changes revert to normal after egg laying.

Habitat and Distribution   A sedentary subspecies that forms permanent pair bond. It frequents and seldom leaves the bare lava rocks of the foreshore. Its breeding range is confined solely to the Galapagos Islands, being partly replaced by or hybridizing with *B.s. striatus*, on Isabela and Santa Cruz.

Chinese Pond Heron

Ardeola bacchus

Description   Length 52 cm. In breeding plumage head and neck dark maroony rufous, with a lanceolate crest growing from nape. Back and a number of scapulars slaty black. Chin and throat white. Long plumes emanating from breast deep chestnut, shading to slaty black towards tips. Wings, tail and rest of body white, with brown tips to the central few primaries. Orbital skin greenish-yellow. Iris deep golden yellow. Bill yellow, shading to blackish towards tip, blue at base. Legs and feet yellowish-green. Female has less developed crest, lacks slaty-black patch on breast and has much paler foreneck. In eclipse plumage both adults have more brown and buff on head and neck, resembling immature birds with their streaky plumage.

Characteristics and Behaviour   In non-breeding plumage very similar to the Indian Pond Heron (*A. grayii*) but slightly larger, and of similar behaviour.

Habitat and Food   As for the Indian Pond Heron.

Display   No information.

Breeding   Nests in small mixed heronries along with the Indian Pond Heron and other species. Season chiefly May to July and on to end of August. Eggs three to five, pale sea green. Size 37.7 × 28.4 mm. Incubation period not known.

Distribution   Resident, with local movement, in eastern Assam, Manipur, Bangladesh and the Andaman Islands. Also breeds in China from Kansu to the Tsingling Mountains, and south to Burma, Thailand, Malaysia, Hainan and Borneo. A wanderer to Japan where breeding has not been recorded.

Lava Heron (*Butorides striatus sundevalli*)

Indian Pond Heron

(Paddybird)

Ardeola grayii

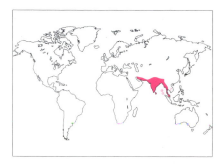

Description Length 46 cm. A strikingly handsome bird in full breeding plumage, with long lanceolate plumes of buff or white draping backwards down the neck forming the occipital crest. The deep brownish-crimson feathers of the back grow very long posteriorly, some of them projecting beyond the tail. Tail and wings white, with brownish-tinged tips to first primaries. Head and neck pale yellowish-brown, crown somewhat browner. Chin and throat white; the long feathers of upper breast greyish-brown. Iris lemon yellow. Bill greenish-yellow, blue at base. Legs dull green. Sexes alike at all times. Non-breeding attire (more often seen) much drabber; head and neck dark brown with yellow-brown streaks; back, scapulars and tertiaries ashy brown; scapulars have pale yellow shaft stripes. The Maldivian Pond Heron (*A.g. phillipsi*) is similar in size, plumage and behaviour.

Characteristics and Bahaviour In flight, a very prominent bird because of the predominantly snow-white plumage, which, surprisingly, blends in with its surroundings when at rest with wings folded. Flies with neck partially extended (not retracted as the Grey Heron, *Ardea cinerea*) and on leisurely flapping wings. Egret-like in many respects.

Habitat At the coast and in the plains, up to altitudes of 1200 m in the peninsular hills, and 1500 m in the valleys of Kashmir and Nepal. Frequents marshes, streams, flooded paddy fields, even stagnant roadside ditches and puddles, also tidal mudflats. *A.g. phillipsi* favours freshwater ponds, and even rain puddles, also tidal mudflats.

Food Hunts in a heron-like fashion, lifting each foot clear of the water with every stride, as it slowly and stealthily stalks its prey, or stands hunched and motionless at the water's edge, keenly alert with bill held in readiness for the catch. Usually a lone feeder or with but a few others of its kind and then always quite well spaced. After the monsoon rains large numbers may be seen feeding collectively at drying-up village ponds. Included in the diet are frogs, fish (mudskippers from tidal swamps), crustaceans (including crabs) on sandy shores; also water beetles and various other insects.

Voice When flushed a harsh croak. Nesting colonies are alive with the continuous 'wa-koo wa-koo' delivered in an almost human-like conversational manner.

Display Not recorded.

Breeding In most parts of India and Pakistan the season extends from May to September; southern India November to February; Sri Lanka November to August. Usually in small colonies with other pond herons, at other times in a mixed colony with night herons, and not necessarily close to water. The untidy platform of twigs may be constructed in a large isolated tree, or even a clump of tamarind or mango, quite regularly in the middle of a small town or village. Sometimes in willows growing from water. Three to four sea-green eggs are laid, size 38 × 28.5 mm. Both sexes help build the nest, share the incubation (24 days), and later feed the young (by regurgitation), the young birds grabbing hold of the adult's bill, as is usual with

Indian Pond Heron (*Ardeola grayii*)
non-breeding plumage

heron species. Although it has not been proved, the Indian Pond Heron is said to pair for life.

Distribution Throughout India, Pakistan and Sri Lanka; the Andaman, Nicobar and Laccadive Islands. Also from the Persian Gulf to Burma and Malaysia. The birds are resident but move around locally as drought or flood dictates. *A.g. phillipsi* is peculiar to the Maldive Islands, occurring on the southernmost atolls: Addu and Suadiva.

Malagasy Pond Heron
(Madagascar Squacco Heron)

Ardeola idae

Description Length 45 cm. Breeding plumage entirely snow white with long filamentous plumes on breast and back, and short crest feathers. Lores greenish, with a suggestion of red on orbital skin in front of eye. Iris yellow. Bill sky blue, broadly tipped with black. Legs dull rosy pink; feet fawny green. Sexes alike. Non-breeding plumage very like other pond herons; bill greenish-grey and tipped black; legs greeny grey.

Habitat and Distribution Favours shallow waters, either fresh, saline or brackish, but requires adequate vegetative cover and the close proximity of trees or bushes. A bulky platform of sticks and twigs is constructed in a tree, usually at a higher level than those of other species within a mixed colony. Once distributed throughout Madagascar, but now rare or absent in parts, being most often seen in western coastal regions. Migrates to eastern and central Africa, where it is seen regularly from May to October; also visits eastern Zaire.

Squacco Heron

Ardeola ralloides

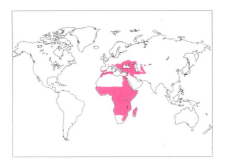

Description Length 46 cm. In the breeding season crown and neck yellowish-buff, superimposed by black-edged white feathers that form a long mane which reaches the mantle. Mantle, scapulars and tertials pinkish-brown; the long golden plumes of the mantle falling elegantly over the pure white wings, rump and tail. The rich golden buff of chest and foreneck display a pleasing contrast with the white of chin and remainder of underparts. Bare loral skin bright yellowish-green. Iris yellow. The rather short legs and the feet are reddish-pink in the early part of breeding season, coinciding with the bright lores. Bill sharp, green or blue over the basal half, the remainder dark brown or even black. Non-breeding plumage somewhat duller, almost brown above, with a shortened mane; underparts streaked and sullied white; bill and loral skin duller; legs and feet yellowish-green. Sexes alike.

Characteristics and Behaviour Appears brownish-buff when standing, but on taking to the air the gleaming white of the wings, rump and tail is exposed. Looks similar to the Cattle Egret (*Bubulcus ibis*) but is less white with a more pointed bill. It walks freely and can climb extremely well. It is active during the day although it is more skulking and secretive in its actions than either the *Egretta* species or the Cattle Egret. It is mostly solitary, hunting at dusk or night-time, but on migration large flocks do occur.

Habitat Favours abundant reed cover, and a scattering of bushes or trees that shroud areas of fresh shallow water. Unfortunately much of this type of habitat is coming under attack from agriculture. During the winter migration brackish and coastal waters are also frequented.

Food A solitary and crepuscular hunter, stalking its prey slowly and seizing it with swift jabs of the sharp bill. A large proportion of its diet consists of insects (up to 80%), including dragonflies, grasshoppers and butterflies. It has been observed standing on water lilies and capturing fish as they feed on small creatures attached to the underside of the leaves.

Voice Even for a heron it is singularly quiet, uttering a harsh but high-pitched single note at dusk, or if alarmed. Its display is accompanied by a kind of 'caw' or 'croaking' sound.

Display Courtship activities involve the raising of every single plume to such an extent as to almost double its normal size. The courting male follows this with a 'stretch display', bobbing up and down and producing the 'cawing' or 'croaking' sound.

Breeding As a general rule the Squacco Heron is a colonial breeder, often mixing with other species. The nest is a solid construction of dead reeds, only occasionally incorporating sticks, situated in low trees below the surrounding nests of other species, often almost on the ground and only 1 m or so above water level. In southern Africa and Madagascar the clutch consists of three to four, or only two eggs, whereas in Europe four to six eggs are invariably laid. They are greenish-blue in colour and a little darker than those of the Cattle Egret, measuring 39 × 28 mm. European eggs

Squacco Heron (*Ardeola ralloides*)

are laid from mid-May to early June; slightly earlier in Africa. Incubation takes about 22 days in Europe; but in the Tsimbazaza heronry, Africa, around 18 days is recorded. Incubating the eggs and caring for the young are shared by both birds, and the chicks are fed at first by regurgitation, and later by food deposited at the nest.

Distribution The breeding range is not as extensive as that of other herons. It breeds almost throughout the entire African continent, with the exception of the Sahara and the extreme south west. In Madagascar it breeds alongside the Malagasy Pond Heron (*A. idae*). In Asia it is fairly common in its range which extends only slightly east of the Aral Sea, from the Caspian Sea westwards

through Asia Minor, and into south-east Europe as far as Yugoslavia and Hungary. It has a rather scattered and patchy distribution in western Europe, where it is confined to the Po valley in Italy, and breeds in only two small areas in France, one of which is the famous Carmargue reserve. Breeding occurs in the Iberian Peninsula, especially in its southern portion, with the largest stronghold probably being in the Coto Donaña reserve. Populations south of the Sahara are resident, but from the breeding grounds of North Africa, Asia and Europe, birds migrate over the Sahara to winter in equatorial Africa, the swamps of West Africa and the inundated zone of the Niger River. Coupled with the resident birds this migratory influx makes the bird extremely numerous in its winter quarters.

Rufous-bellied Heron

Ardeola rufiventris
(Butorides rufiventris)

Description Length 39 cm. Male
very dark slaty grey with deep chestnut
belly, rump, tail and shoulder patches.
Lores and orbital skin yellow. Iris yellow
or golden orange. Bill, upper mandible
dark horny brown, most of lower mandible yellow, blackish at tip. Female similar, but the dark grey plumage is tinged
with sooty brown and a buffish stripe
extends down the foreneck from the base
of the chin. Lores and orbital skin very
pale yellow. Bill, lower mandible greenish or orange-yellow for basal two-
thirds.

Habitat and Distribution Inhabits
dense reed beds or flooded grasslands
with trees in close proximity. Breeds colonially, building a platform of sticks in
shrubs or low trees about 1 m or so above
the ground; also nests in dense reed beds.
Occurs southwards from the equatorial
rain forests of West Africa, and no further north than the Sudan in East Africa.
Some of the principal breeding areas are
in the region of the Kafue River in Zambia, the Zambezi valley, the Okavango
delta and almost certainly the swampy
regions between Tanzania and Rwanda
formed by the Kagera River.

Javanese Pond Heron
Ardeola speciosa

Description Length 46 cm. When in non-breeding plumage is so like the Chinese and Indian Pond Herons (*A. bacchus* and *A. grayii*) as to be indistinguishable. In breeding plumage head, crest and neck pale golden orange, with basal neck collar and long breast plumes tending towards dull cinnamon. Mantle and scapulars brownish-black. Rest of plumage, including underparts and chin, white. Lores dull greenish-yellow. Iris yellow or orange. Bill yellow with broad black tip. Legs greenish-yellow when breeding, later becoming dark greenish. Sexes alike. *A.s. continentalis* may be differentiated only by larger size of wing and bill.

Habitat and Distribution Frequents the margins of lakes and ponds, also paddy fields, flooded grasslands, mangrove swamps and coastal mudflats. Nests solitary or in small groups from December to June, but mainly during January and February. Breeds Borneo, the Celebes, Sumatra, Java, also Karimunjawa and Sumbawa in the Lesser Sunda Islands, southern Vietnam, Kampuchea, central Thailand, southern Indochina and Tenasserim in south-east Burma. *A.s. continentalis* is probably restricted to the mainland.

Cattle Egret
Bubulcus ibis

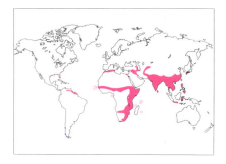

Description Length 51 cm. The long hair-like tufts of golden-buff feathers on head, neck, chest and back make it unmistakable in the breeding season, although at a distance it may appear wholly white. Orbital and facial skin greenish-yellow. Iris yellow. Bill yellowish. Legs and feet black, upper parts of tibia yellowish. Non-breeding plumage pure white. Sexes alike.

Characteristics and Behaviour Usually seen from some little distance and almost always in the company of grazing cattle, not always near to water. Very like the Little Egret (*Egretta garzetta*) in non-breeding plumage, but is always distinguishable by bill colour which is yellowish (rather than black as in the Little Egret). In flight the neck is folded back, the head is drawn in between the shoulders, and the legs project beyond the tail. Every evening they proceed to their favourite trees to roost.

Habitat Frequents open plains, cultivated farmland and grazing pastures. Also fairly high plateaux and peninsular hills which they often visit daily from lower-lying land.

Food Forages around the legs of grazing cattle for grasshoppers and other insects disturbed by the cattle. Also can often be seen standing on the backs of grazing animals picking off ticks, blood-sucking flies and other parasitic insects. Often gather to feed in large flocks when the fields are being ploughed, picking for insects in the newly tilled earth. Earthworms, carabid beetles and flies are all included in the diet; feeds less frequently on lizards, tadpoles and frogs.

Voice Not a very vocal species. A low croak is used at the nesting colony.

Display Not recorded.

Breeding Nests colonially in large trees along with other species such as cormorants or night herons, or in small to medium-sized colonies comprised entirely of its own kind, and not necessarily close to water. Both sexes share in nest construction. Eggs three to five, very pale glaucous or almost white. Size 44 × 36.5 mm. Incubation period not known but shared by both sexes as is feeding of the young. In northern India eggs are laid from June to August; in the south November to February; in Sri Lanka from February to July. In southern Europe, North African coastal areas and United States, probably March, April or May.

Distribution Breeds in Portugal, southern Spain, Morocco, Algeria, Egypt, tropical Africa and Madagascar, along the east coast of the USA, the greater Antilles, Venezuela and Guyana. A vagrant to Britain, Denmark, Hungary, the Balkans and France (where it has been known to breed). The subspecies *B.i. coromandus* breeds and is resident throughtout India, Pakistan, Sri Lanka, the Andaman, Nicobar and Maldive Islands. Those in the Himalayas migrate to lower land in winter. Also breeds in Burma, Indochina, Korea, south China, Malaysia, south Japan, Taiwan, Hainan, the Philippines, the Sunda Islands, the Celebes, Ceram and the central east coast of Australia. *B.i. seychellarum* breeds in the Seychelles.

Cattle Egret (*Bubulcus ibis*)

38

Great Egret

(American Egret or Great White Heron)

Egretta alba (Casmerodius albus)

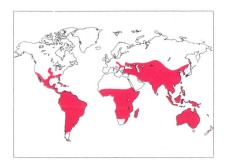

Description Length 96–103 cm. A large snow-white heron-like bird, smaller than the American Great White Heron (*Ardea herodias occidentalis*) and with different leg colour. During the breeding season a large spray of filamentous plumes (aigrettes) develops on the back (not the head), extending over and beyond the tail. Neck and head long and slender. Bill pointed, black with yellow base in summer; yellow in winter. Legs greenish-black, upper part of tibia pinkish-orange in breeding season. Sexes alike. The Eastern Large Egret (*E.a. modesta*) is a slightly smaller subspecies (length 91 cm) but is otherwise indistinguishable from the nominate.

Characteristics and Behaviour Outside the breeding season tends to be a solitary species with behaviour and feeding habits very much as the Grey Heron (*Ardea cinerea*). In flight, the wing beat is slow but deliberate, with neck and head pulled in close to the shoulders and legs trailing out beyond the tail.

Habitat Enjoys fairly open but shallow fresh water such as ponds and the margins of lakes; also seen along rivers. The brackish waters of swamps are also frequented, as are saltwater habitats such as tidal estuaries etc.

Food Diet includes all manner of aquatic animals, fish and frogs; also small mammals, snakes and various water insects.

Voice During displays and in the nesting period an occasional throaty croak, 'frawnk'.

Display Not fully documented. During nest ceremonies in the breeding season, the plumes on its back are often erected and spread out, forming a diaphanous showering filigree.

Breeding A colonial nester; in parts of its range it joins mixed colonies with storks, cormorants and darters. The nest is either a scant, loosely constructed platform in a tree, or a mound of material in a reed bed which has built up over the years. It may or may not be lined. The male sometimes repairs or constructs the nest before arrival of female. Eggs three to four, measuring 54.6 × 38.6 mm and pale bluish-green. Those of *E.a. modesta* slightly smaller at 54 × 38.6 mm. The breeding season may commence at the end of March and continue on into May. With *E.a. modesta* December to May in Sri Lanka; July to September in Sind and Northern India; further south in India November to February.

Distribution Breeds in south-east Europe, central Asia, Africa south to South Africa and Madagascar. It is suspected that European birds may winter in Africa. *E.a. egretta* breeds in America from eastern Oregon, south-east Minnesota, Lake Erie and southern New Jersey, to southern Chile and southern Argentina. North American breeders retreat in winter to California, southern Arizona, New Mexico, central Texas and the Gulf Coast. In other parts of the world it is a resident, making but local movements as water conditions dictate. The most westerly breeding limits in Europe are Neusiedl (Austria) and the Vilky-Tisy ponds of southern Czechoslovakia. *E.a. modesta* breeds in Pakistan,

40

Great Egret (*Egretta alba*)

India, Sri Lanka, Burma, China, Korea, Japan, Indonesia, Malaysia and Australia. Also resident within the breeding range making local movement with changing water conditions.

It is no surprise that the species became very rare in parts of Europe and North America at the turn of the century. Countless thousands of these birds were killed for their plumes or 'aigrettes' to adorn ladies' hats and dresses. It is estimated that in 1902 alone some 200,000 birds were slaughtered in areas close to the fashion conscious cities of Europe and the USA. *E.a. maorianus* breeds South Island, New Zealand. *E.a. melanorhynchus* breeds Senegal to Sudan and Cape Province.

41

Black Heron

Egretta ardesiaca

Description Length 48–50 cm. Plumage entirely black, with elongated plumes of crown and nape forming a crest, and lanceolate plumes of lower neck falling over upper breast. Iris yellow. Bill and legs black; feet yellow. Sexes alike.

Habitat and Distribution Colonial when breeding. Nests in trees at heights varying from 0.75–6 m above water in mangrove swamps or similar situations. Confined to Africa south of the Sahara, and Madagascar. Season November to January near Durban; February to March on the Wembere; February to June in Madagascar; May to June in the Kisumu heronry; and July to August near Accra.

Little Blue Heron

Egretta caerulea

Description Length 64–74 cm. Predominantly dark grey, but with head and neck dull reddish-grey. Lores dull green, becoming marine blue when breeding. Iris pale yellow. Bill slaty grey with black tip. Legs and feet bluish-grey. Bill and legs darker when breeding. Sexes alike.

Habitat and Distribution Frequents marshes and freshwater lagoons. The nesting platforms are built in mangroves at heights varying from 0.75 to 12 m. Breeds in North America along the eastern coastlands of the Gulfs of California and Mexico. Also the southern Mississippi basin, and south from Long Island along the east coast to Florida. There are large nesting colonies in the swamps of Arkansas, Louisiana and western Tennessee. Also breeds in the West Indies, and south through Central America and South America to Lima (Peru) in the west, and Uruguay in the east.

Black Herons

Swinhoe's Egret
(Chinese Egret)

Egretta eulophotes

Description Length 68 cm. Plumage entirely white, with elongated crest plumes up to 11.5 cm long when breeding. Also long breast plumes, and dorsal plumes extending beyond tail. Very like the white form of Eastern Reef Heron (*E. sacra*), but can only be confused in winter when their ranges overlap. Lores bright blue. Iris yellow. Bill yellow, becoming orange-yellow when breeding. Legs black; feet yellow (in breeding birds). Sexes alike.

Habitat and Distribution Frequents mudflats and shallow tidal estuaries. Nests reported to be built in shrubs and constructed from dry grass (North Korea), or platform nests of sticks in tall trees (Hong Kong). Nowadays a very rare species, with Perak on west coast of Malay Peninsula, Selangor, and Singapore within its present-day breeding range.

43

Little Egret

Egretta garzetta

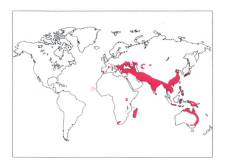

Description Length 63 cm. A snow-white bird similar to, but smaller than, the Great Egret (*E. alba*) and the Intermediate Egret (*E. intermedia*). However, when in breeding plumage it not only has long filamentous plumes of feathers on its back and breast, but also displays two long narrow drooping plumes on the nape. Facial skin greenish-yellow. Iris yellow. Bill black, the base of lower mandible yellowish. Legs black but feet yellow or greenish-yellow. Sexes alike.

Characteristics and Behaviour Quite similar to the Cattle Egret (*Bubulcus ibis*) in non-breeding plumage, but distinguishable at all times by the black and yellow bill and colour of legs and feet. Both the Cattle Egret and the Squacco Heron (*Ardeola ralloides*) appear white at a distance, but are stockier built birds with thicker necks and shorter bills. More gregarious than either the Great or Intermediate Egret. Flies in the manner usual to egrets, flapping slowly but steadily, with neck drawn into shoulders. Can be found roosting in trees along with other species.

Habitat Favours marshes, swampy areas and lagoons. Much less likely to be encountered on coastal mudflats or the seashore.

Food Stalks its prey in typical heron-like fashion, lungeing out with neck and pointed bill to catch hold of its quarry. Fish, frogs, crustaceans and aquatic insects are all part of its diet.

Voice The occasional deep croak along with other guttural outbursts, but mostly a very silent bird.

Display Displays of greeting, by one bird for its mate during visits to the nest, are accompanied by loud croaks and gargling noises. They also involve pointing the bill vertically upwards, followed by drawing in and stretching out the neck repeatedly. This often encourages reciprocal displays from occupants of neighbouring nests.

Breeding A colonial nester in mixed heronries. The nest is a loosely constructed platform of twigs, in trees at heights of 2–6 m. They are often built very close together and on occasions even touch those of different species. Favourite sites are flooded tamarisk forests and partially submerged trees in monsoon flooded jungle. A normal clutch would be three to five pale blue-green eggs. Size 44.4 × 32 mm. Both sexes share the incubation for 21–25 days. Feeding and caring for the young is also undertaken by both adults. In the northern hemisphere first eggs are laid in early April; in Sind (Pakistan) and northern India, July to September; in southern India, November to February; Sri Lanka, December to May. The times depend considerably on water conditions.

Distribution Breeds in southern and eastern Europe (including south-west Spain, southern France, Italy and Yugoslavia), North and East Africa, the Middle East, Iran, Afghanistan, Pakistan, India and the Himalayas (Nepal valley). Also Sri Lanka, the Andaman, Nicobar, Laccadive and Maldive Islands, Burma, Malaysia, China, Hainan, Japan, the Philippines, New Guinea, Java, and the north, east and south-east of Australia from Melbourne

44

Little Egret (*Egretta garzetta*) with one
Great Egret

to Darwin. Usually a resident bird moving locally with water conditions.

The 'dark form' of the Little Egret is
found only on the island of Madagascar
and Aldabra. It can be distinguished
from the Black Heron (*E. ardesiaca*) by its
smaller size, white chin and throat.

Intermediate Egret
(Smaller, Yellow-billed or Median Egret)

Egretta intermedia

Description Length 45 cm. Pure white and very like the Eastern Large Egret (*E. alba modesta*) but somewhat smaller. The presence of filamentous plumes of feathers on back and breast is diagnostic during the breeding season, at which time the bill is black with yellow base. Non-breeding birds have lemon-yellow bill with dusky tip, browny at base. Legs and feet blackish, but greenish on the joints and tibia (no colour change of legs recorded in breeding birds). Iris lemon yellow. Naked lores and infra-orbital skin yellowish-green when breeding; yellowish in non-breeders. Sexes alike.

Characteristics and Behaviour Not quite as gregarious as the Little Egret (*E. garzetta*) but occasionally seen in small parties even outside breeding season. In other ways very like the Great Egret (*E. alba*).

Habitat Low country and also plateaux up to 1400 m. It frequents marshes, mangrove swamps and flooded meadows; also coastal backwaters and tidal estuaries.

Food Similar to the Great Egret.

Voice and Display Not recorded.

Breeding A colonial nesting species, quite often in mixed heronries. The nest is typical of the egrets, just a loosely constructed platform of twigs in a tree, not necessarily close to water and often in a small town or village. Favourite nesting sites are the flooded tamarisk forests of Sind (Pakistan), and the tidal mangrove swamps in Kutch and in other coastal areas. The three to five pale glaucous eggs measure 47.6 × 35.8 mm, and are laid from July to September in Sind and northern India; November to February further south; and December to May in Sri Lanka. Both sexes share the incubation for a period of 21–25 days, and the feeding and caring for the young.

Distribution Breeds and is resident throughout Pakistan, India, Sri Lanka, the Andaman and Nicobar Islands, making only local movements corresponding with water conditions. Also breeds in Burma, Thailand, Indochina, Malaysia, east to China and Japan, south to the Greater Sunda Islands, Papua-New Guinea and the Philippines, where it is resident in some areas but migratory in others. *E.i. plumifera* breeds in South Moluccas, New Guinea and Australia. *E.i. brachyrhyncha* breeds in Africa from the Sudan to Cape Province.

Western Reef Heron
Egretta gularis

Description Length 63 cm. Two colour phases: one pure white, the other darker, varying from slaty grey to slaty blue-black but with throat and upperparts of foreneck white. When in breeding plumage has a nuchal crest comprising two long narrow plumes, and filamentous plumes on breast and back. There are also birds with plumage intermediate between the white and dark phases. Iris yellow. In white phase, bill

Intermediate Egret (*Egretta intermedia*)

yellowish at base and on lower mandible, upper mandible horny brown; legs greenish-black; feet and toes yellowish. In dark phase, bill mainly bright yellow; legs greenish-black; feet and toes yellowish-brown. Sexes alike. The India Reef Heron (*E.g. asha*; often referred to as *E.g. schistacea*) and the Mascarene Reef Heron (*E.g. dimorpha*) are both similar to the nominate. *E.g. dimorpha* has two colour phases and is slightly smaller than the nominate at 56 cm long.

Characteristics and Behaviour
Apart from its more solitary habit and its fondness for the sea coast, the white phase is indistinguishable from the Little Egret (*E. garzetta*), with the same general behaviour and flight. Gregarious during breeding season.

47

Habitat Frequents both sandy and rocky coastal regions; also mudflats, tidal lagoons and mangrove swamps. Only occasionally does it visit freshwater swamps away from the coast.

Food Feeds in shallow surf on the incoming or receding tide, and amongst the rock pools left behind. Food items acquired by jabbing action of pointed bill as bird wades (often belly-deep) in water. Fish, crabs and molluscs are taken. Another regular item taken from tidal mud is the mudskipper.

Voice Mainly a silent bird, uttering the occasional throaty croak.

Display Supplants rival birds by running towards them. When fighting, opponents will fly at each other, rising a little distance above ground, and with crown feathers raised will jab out with bill.

Breeding Usually in colonies comprised of own species, but also in mixed ones with pond herons, night herons and other species of egret. In north-west Africa the season extends from spring to autumn, with eggs being laid between April and September. Mainly June to August in Red Sea regions. Breeding season for *E.g. asha* April to August in Sind and Kutch, late May in Sri Lanka. The nest is an untidy platform of sticks (sometimes including new wood still in leaf), built in a large tree, the colony itself often continuing into neighbouring trees. A typical site would be a tidal mangrove swamp. Both colour phases breed in the same colony, often interbreeding (except in the case of *E.g. asha*). Eggs three or four, pale blue-green in colour and very similar to those of the Little Egret. Size 45 × 34 mm. Incubation commences with first egg and is shared by both sexes; period undetermined (probably 21–25 days). Young are fed by regurgitation.

Distribution Breeds in southern extremities of the western Palearctic, on several islands, Banc d'Arguin, in Egypt on Red Sea coast. Also Iraq, Kuwait, and various islands such as Kubbar, Bubiyan, Warba; also Auha and coastal areas of north-west Africa. *E.g. asha* breeds along the northern coast of Saudi Arabia; very common in coastal regions of Pakistan; the western coast of India and south to Kanyakumaria; north-west Sri Lanka; and the Laccadive Islands. *E.g. dimorpha* certainly breeds on Aldabra, Cosmoledo and Astove; also throughout Madagascar (except forest and dry savanna regions), where the white form/black form ratio is 2 to 1.

Reddish Egret
Egretta rufescens

Description Length 69–81 cm. Principally a grey bird with reddish-brown neck and head (although on occasions the bird is completely grey, and very occasionally entirely reddish-black). When breeding, lanceolate plumes develop on head and neck giving bird a 'shaggy' appearance. Lores pinkish-mauve, changing to bright violet when breeding. Iris pale buff. Bill pink with blackish tip. Legs and feet greyish-blue. Sexes alike but female slightly smaller. *E.r. dickeyi* has head and neck almost chocolate brown and *E.r. colorata* is larger than the nominate with a browner head and neck.

Habitat and Distribution Seldom wanders far from sea coasts and tidal estuaries. A platform nest of twigs is constructed in a tree at heights of up to 3 m. Breeds in southern Texas, where the population is estimated at 14,000–16,000 pairs, in July/August. In Florida breeds the year round but principally November to January, and February to April/May. Also breeds West Indies and Central America. *E.r. dickeyi* breeds San Luis Island, Gulf of California. *E.r. colorata* breeds Mexico along central and southern Pacific coasts.

Eastern Reef Heron
(Pacific Reef Egret)
Egretta sacra

Description Length 58 cm. Dimorphic, being either pure white, or dark slaty grey or slaty black; the dark phase having a streak of white running down middle of chin and throat. Both forms have a bushy crest of feathers growing from nape of neck, also long lanceolate feathers on lower neck hanging over breast, and similar long plumes on back that reach to middle of tail. These shade to a paler grey than the rest of the plumage in the dark phase birds. Bill very stout, upper mandible horny brown, yellowish at base, lower mandible yellowish. In some instances the white form has an all yellow bill. Iris yellow. Legs of white birds pale greenish-yellow, the darker phase birds have legs dull dusky green to almost black. Sexes alike.

Eastern Reef Heron

Characteristics and Behaviour A little smaller than the Western Reef Heron (*E. gularis*) but distinguishable in breeding plumage by the crest: the Western has two lanceolate plumes as opposed to the bushy crest of the Eastern. A solitary bird which spends long periods at high water perched on partly submerged rocks awaiting the ebb.

Habitat Frequents mudflats at low water; also favours rocky stretches of coastline.

Food Wades in rock pools left by the tide, or the shallow water on an ebbing tide, stalking fish (especially mudskippers) and crabs. Above the high water mark will sometimes feed on insects, such as grasshoppers.

Voice When alarmed a long harsh 'arrrk'. During bouts of feeding the occasional croak which seems to follow a successful catch. At other times usually silent.

Display Not recorded.

Breeding The nest is an untidy platform of sticks and twigs built in rock crevices and hollows, often in a small fig tree or among mangrove trees in a creek, at heights of up to 1 m above water level. The eggs number three or four and are pale sea green in colour. Size 44.8 × 33.3 mm. Incubation probably continues for 21–25 days and is shared by both sexes, as is the feeding of the young.

Distribution Breeds and is resident in the Andaman and Nicobar Islands. Also breeds on the eastern coasts of the Bay of Bengal and east to Burma, in Malaysia, south-east China, Hainan, Taiwan, Japan, Korea, Sunda Islands, the Philippines and Moluccas, Celebes, New Guinea, South Pacific Islands, north Australia and New Zealand. *E.s. albolineata* breeds New Caledonia.

Snowy Egret
Egretta thula

Description Length 56–66 cm. A pure white egret, smaller than the Great Egret (*E. alba*) and Little Egret (*E. garzetta*). Bare facial skin yellow, flushes

a reddish or pale pink during nuptial phase; also at this time it acquires a tuft of nuchal plumes. This tuft of plumes and the recurved dorsal plumes are distinguishing features. Bill dark coloured. Legs black; toes bright yellow (greenish-yellow in Little Egret). Sexes alike but female smaller. *E.g. brewsteri* is very similar but larger than the nominate.

Habitat and Distribution When nesting or feeding favours areas bordered or flooded by water, although areas of bush or dry grassland are also visited at these times. Does not restrict itself to fresh water only (as the Cattle Egret, *Bubulcus ibis*), in fact in some areas it shows a decided tendency towards salt or brackish water habitats. The breeding season is earlier in the north than in the south. March to May are peak periods in the USA and Puerto Rico; November to January in Ecuador and Chile. A stick platform is usually constructed about 3 m above ground. Clutch size usually three to five. A widespread species throughout the Americas from about 42°N to 40°S. Nesting is now frequent along the Utah/Idaho border in the west, and on Long Island in the east where the first nest was found in 1953. Locally numerous in Central and South America, but has not yet regained its former abundance in the Caribbean Islands. *E.t. brewsteri* breeds in the western third of the USA and north Mexico.

Tricoloured Heron
(Louisiana Heron)

Egretta tricolor

Description Length 60–70 cm. Head, neck, wings and tail slaty blue. Long filamentous plumes on mantle, and scapulars tinged reddish-brown when breeding. Chin, throat and foreneck white, with a central brownish stripe down latter. Two or three white plumes on crown during breeding season. Lower breast, belly, tail and underwings white. When breeding, lores change from yellowish to pale mauve; iris from reddish-brown to scarlet; bill changes from browny yellow to bright blue with dusky tip; and the greenish-yellow legs become deep pink. Sexes alike but female a little smaller. *E.t. rufiventrum* has a rufous chin.

Habitat and Distribution Frequents mangrove swamps, coastal mudflats, freshwater swamps and riverbanks. A colonial nester, often in mixed colonies. Nest, a platform of sticks, built at heights up to 3 m above ground. Breeds on the west coast of America from San Diego (including Gulf of California), south to northern limits of Peru. On the east coast from Long Island, south via the Caribbean Islands and Gulf of Mexico, to the Amazon mouth. *E.t. ruficollis* breeds West Indies; *E.t. rufiventrum* breeds in Trinidad.

Snowy Egret

Slaty Egret

Egretta vinaceigula

Description Length 43 cm. Plumage mainly pale bluish-grey, but throat pale cinnamon. Flanks and abdomen blackish. Iris pale yellow, with ring of black feathers around eye. Bill long, slaty black and pointed. Legs and feet dull greyish-yellow. Sexes alike but female slightly smaller.

Habitat and Distribution Colonial, nesting in reed beds. Range in north-west Botswana thought to be through the swamps and flooded plains of the Okavango, and northwards to similar habitats in the Chobe National Park, also Namibia (in the Caprivi Strip) and the Transvaal.

Agami Heron
(Chestnut-bellied Heron)

Agamia agami

Description Length 71 cm on average. Head, neck, breast and underparts rich chestnut. Nape, crest and wispy hackles of lower neck pale grey. Chin, throat and narrow band down front of upper neck white. Back, wings and tail blackish with deep metallic green gloss. A few elongated plumes on lower back have long pale grey tips. Bare facial skin yellowish-green. Iris reddish-brown. Bill long 14 cm (often longer) and rapier-like, pale blue, but tip and culmen black. Legs and feet yellow. Female somewhat smaller.

Habitat and Distribution Frequents dense swampy woodlands. Deeply cupped platform nests have been found in trees standing in water, with the nest itself 1.3–2 m above water level. Breeds in Central and South America, from eastern Mexico to northern and eastern parts of Bolivia; also in Brazil along the upper reaches of rivers flowing from the Mato Grosso.

Capped Heron

Pilherodius pileatus

Description Length 51–59 cm. Plumage mainly white with a suggestion of pale grey in feathers of back and wings. Black cap does not include forehead, the latter being white. Growing from nape are two or three extremely long white plumes, 20 cm in length, which usually hang over the back. A buffish suffusion occurs on areas of neck, breast and wings when breeding; this is probably due to the application of powder, from the powder-down patches, during preening. Lores and orbital skin bright blue. Bill cobalt blue with pearly-grey tip, but much variation occurs. Legs and feet ashy grey in male; blue-grey in female. Sexes alike.

Habitat and Distribution Favours watery situations, tropical rain forests, swampy forest regions, flooded paddy fields, also requires thick vegetative cover into which it may retreat. The nest is a platform of sticks in a small tree, or on lower branches of a quite tall tree. A rather rare species throughout the South American tropics, where it ranges from Panama southwards into Bolivia and south-east Brazil, and eastwards to the mouth of the Amazon, including Colombia, Venezuela, Guyana, Surinam and French Guiana.

Capped Heron

Whistling Heron

Syrigma sibilatrix

Description Length 53–61 cm. Cap black, with long black, yellow-tipped plumes. Throat white. Lower face pale rufous. Neck and long plumes overhanging breast rufous yellow. Back and wings grey; the pale rufous feathers of wing coverts broadly edged with dark brown. Breast, belly, flanks and rump pale yellow. Lores blue, tinged violet at base. Iris pale yellow. Bill dull pink, becoming dusky towards tip. Legs and feet black or blackish-brown. Sexes alike. *S.s. fostersmithi* is a little smaller, has a longer bill and less streaked wing coverts.

Habitat and Distribution Occurs in open marshy grassland, lagoons and the margins of estuaries and creeks; also open forests with ponds and pools. The platform nest is built in a tree, usually out on a branch and at a height of 3–6 m. Usually a solitary breeder, peak season being January. Occurs southwards from Bolivia, south-east Brazil and Paraguay, to Buenos Aires in Argentina. The northern subspecies, *S.s. fostersmithi*, occurs in Venezuela and Colombia in the region of the upper Orinoco River.

Boat-billed Heron

Cochlearius cochlearius

Description   Length 45–50 cm. The black crown contrasts against the white of forehead and cheeks. Broad black lanceolate plumes droop from the nape over the back. The buffy-brown mantle is offset by grey wings and merges into a vinaceous colour on the sides of the neck. Upper breast white, lower breast and belly rich rufous. Flanks and feathered tibia black. Only when distended is the gular pouch visible and is described as being dark sulphur yellow in Venezuelan birds, but a distinct pink in the breeding population of Brazil. The bare grey lores and orbital skin are offset by a greenish-yellow spot on the eyelid. Iris 'wood brown'. The characteristic slipper-like bill is black, with base of lower mandible having a yellowish cast. Legs greenish, becoming yellow in the breeding season. Sexes alike.

Characteristics and Behaviour
Bears a certain resemblance to the Night Heron (*Nycticorax nycticorax*) but has black rather than white ribbon-like nape plumes, and a brown instead of black mantle. When standing with the slipper-like bill resting on its breast, or sitting hunched on a shaded branch, it is quite unmistakable.

Habitat   Frequents wooded or mangrove fringes of freshwater creeks, lakes and flooded marshland; preferably with the presence of thick bushes and foliage that overhang the water, providing an ideal roosting and nesting habitat.

Food   Feeding depends wholly on its sensitive bill which is placed below the water surface ready, at the slightest touch, to open and draw inside water, mud and prey, after which it snaps shut instantly. The diet consists of shrimps, fish, or any other small aquatic creatures. Usually a nocturnal feeder, but may also feed in daylight hours when in deep shade.

Voice   At any hour of the day or night a loud, discordant, frog-like croak is uttered. Courtship activities are accompanied by low pitched and seemingly mechanical notes which have great carrying power through the dense vegetation.

Display   Mutual preening, especially of crest feathers, and bill clapping are particularly emphasised during courtship. Even without contact of the mandibles bill clappering can appear most aggressive and is often performed whilst one of the pair is in flight.

Breeding   Breeding either solitary or in small groups, forming mixed heronries. The nest is placed 2–10 m above ground in a tree or bush. It is quite a smallish construction of sticks, although old nests are often enlarged or the old nests of larger species used. Two to four pale blue eggs (usually three) are laid, often spotted with cinnamon at the larger end. Size 50 × 35 mm. Breeding season is determined by rainfall and the availability of food. Incubation is for a period of 25–35 days with both birds sharing the task. At first the young are fed entirely at night-time.

Distribution   Breeding range extends from the coasts of north-central Mexico, south to Peru, Bolivia and north-eastern Argentina. Owing to the vast expanse of country over which it occurs, distinct populations have evolved which can be divided into two groups: the white-breasted birds of the nominate which are found throughout most of South America with the exception of the north-west coast and reaching eastern Panama, and the buffy-brown breasted and usually darker birds of Central America. These have been separated into four subspecies. *C.c. zeledoni* which is thought to be restricted to the west coast of Mexico from Sinaloa to Guerrero. *C.c. panamensis* which is distributed throughout Panama, except for the south-east, and down the Pacific coast of South America to Lima. *C.c. phillipsi* which breeds in northern Guatemala, along the Caribbean slopes from the latitude of Ciudad Victoria in Mexico to the tip of the Yucatán Peninsula, and south to Belize. *C.c. ridgwayi* of the Guatemalan coastlands from Chiapas through El Salvador and western Honduras.

Nankeen Night Heron
(Rufous Night Heron)

Nycticorax caledonicus

Description Length 59 cm. Crown and nape black, with long white nuchal plumes. Face and neck in light shades of chestnut, paling on upper breast. Back, wings and tail dull chestnut. Lower breast and remaining underparts whitish, sometimes washed with pale chestnut. Lores yellowish-green. Iris yellow. A narrow band of white extends from base of bill over and round to rear of eye. Bill mainly black, base of lower mandible greenish. Legs yellowish-green, often becoming pink during courtship. Sexes alike.

Habitat and Distribution Frequents the wooded margins of swamps. A colonial nester, building its platform of sticks on a horizontal branch usually overhanging water. Found in Australia

Boat-billed Heron (*Cochlearius cochlearius*)

wherever swampland occurs. also New Caledonia, and near Blenheim (South Island of New Zealand). *N.c. manillensis* occurs on Manila (the Philippines); *N.c. mandibularis* on Aola and Guadolcanal (the Solomons); *N.c. hilli* at Parry's Creek in north-west Australia, New-Guinea, and eastern Indonesia; *N.c. pelewensis* on the Pelew Islands and the Carolines; *N.c. cancrivorus* on Uatom Island (Bismarck Archipelago, off north New Britain). *N.c. minahassae* in the Celebes.

Night Heron
(Black-crowned Night Heron)

Nycticorax nycticorax

Description   Length 58 cm. Back and scapulars black, sheened with metallic green (more so during breeding season). Crown and nape black. Forehead white; narrow white band over eye. Occipital crest black, but with a few long slender white plumes that drape over back. Wings, rump and tail bluish-grey. Underparts mainly white, but flanks ashy grey. Naked lores and orbital skin yellowish-green. Iris ruby red. Bill black, but base and most of lower mandible greenish-yellow (much blacker in breeding birds). Legs and feet dull green, with colour change in breeding season to lemon yellow or pinkish-yellow. Sexes alike.

Characteristics and Behaviour   A mainly black and grey bird, stockily built, with a much stouter bill than the pond herons. Out of breeding season very crepuscular, even nocturnal in its habits. Gregarious at all times, often several hundred birds sharing a daytime roost in the seclusion of dense tree cover. Their posture is hunchbacked with head drawn well into the shoulders, and never a blink from the deep ruby-red eye. The flight is direct and strong with rapid beats of the wing.

Habitat   Frequents the overgrown banks of rivers, ponds and streams; also swampy and marshy areas with dense marginal tree cover. May also be seen in coastal estuaries, tidal creeks and coastal lagoons.

Food   Feeding usually takes place around dusk and dawn, the birds flying to a favourite spot where they actively seek out their prey. Seldom seen standing motionless, in the true heron fashion, when feeding. Daytime foraging is only really practised when there is a nest full of young birds to satisfy. Included in the diet are aquatic insects and their larvae, such as dragonfly nymphs, fish and frogs.

Voice   When flying to or from a feeding area, the occasional raucous 'kwaark' or 'wock'. Older nestlings that are partially fledged become most vociferous, uttering an almost continuous 'click click click' as they impatiently await the arrival of their next meal.

Display   Territories are established by the males within the breeding colonies, and these are strongly defended against would-be intruders. Here the males enact a display which consists of arching the head and neck forward, raising the crest and fluffing out the feathers of neck, breast and back. Then with head lowered down to the feet a 'snap-hiss' sound is produced, often followed by a spell of preening. Pairs greet each other within the territory by bill rubbing and mutual feather nibbling.

Breeding   A colonial nester either in mixed or single-species heronries. Nest material is collected by the male but the nest itself is built by the female. It is an untidy platform of sticks and twigs, often very flimsy, usually constructed in a mangrove or other bush in a watery situation, but sometimes in tall trees a little way from water, at heights of up to 45 m from ground level. Breeds approximately April to May in Europe, Middle East and the Vale of Kashmir; June or July to September in northern India; December to February in southern India; December to September in Sri Lanka. Eggs three to four, pale blue-

Night Heron (*Nycticorax nycticorax*)

green, size 49 × 35 mm. Both sexes share the incubation (for about 21 days) as well as feeding the young.

Distribution Breeds central and southern Europe, the Middle East, parts of Africa, Madagascar, Pakistan, India, Kashmir and Nepal Valleys at 1900 m, Sri Lanka, Andaman and Nicobar Islands, Burma, Thailand, Malaysia, and Indochina; to China and Japan; also Java. European, Middle Eastern and North African birds probably migrate to tropical Africa in winter. In other more easterly countries the bird is possibly resident within its breeding range with but local movements depending on water conditions. In the Americas the nominate is replaced by the subspecies *N.n. hoackli*, which breeds from southern Canada (excluding British Columbia) and south throughout the USA and South America; also the Hawaii Islands. *N.n. obscurus* breeds from southern Peru to Tierra del Fuego. *N.n. falklandicus* breeds Falkland Islands.

Yellow-crowned Night Heron

Nycticorax violaceus

Description Length 55–70 cm. Crown white (yellowish when not breeding). Crest and long narrow cheek patch also white. Rest of head and throat black. Neck, breast and underparts dull medium grey. Feathers on wings, back and tail blackish-grey, broadly edged with pale grey. Lores yellowish-grey becoming dark green when breeding. Iris scarlet. Bill black, yellowish at base of lower mandible. Legs and feet orange-yellow. Sexes alike but female slightly smaller. *N.v. cayannensis* is darker than the nominate; *N.v. bancroft* is paler and has a heavier bill; *N.v. calignis* has the heavy bill of *N.v. bancroft* but is as dark as *N.v. cayannensis*.

Habitat and Distribution A bird with crepuscular habits, frequenting swampy, wooded regions and breeding colonially. The nest platform is usually situated high in a tree. Breeding commences about March in the USA, and goes on to August in the tropics. A coastal bird breeding in the south-eastern states of America; also middle reaches and tributaries of the Mississippi River; up the east coast as far as New York; and even as far south as Panama and the Grenadines. *N.v. cayannensis* is from the north and north-east coasts of South America, also as far west as Panama; *N.v. pauper* is from the Indefatigable Islands, Galapagos Archipelago; *N.v. bancroft* is from Baja California, along the Pacific coast of Central America south to Guatemala, also the West Indies south to Tobago; *N.v. gravirostris* occurs on Socorro Island, Mexico; and *N.v. caliginis* extends south from Panama along the Pacific coast to Peru.

Japanese Night Heron

Gorsachius goisagi

Description Length 49 cm. Head, short crest and rear of neck dull cinnamon. Sides of neck fawn, slightly tinged with cinnamon. Back and wings cinnamon, finely and evenly mottled with dark brown. Foreneck and breast buffish, boldly streaked with reddish-brown. Belly and flanks buff, mottled with brownish. Loral skin yellowish. Iris yellow. Bill, upper mandible dark brown, lower sullied yellow. Front of legs and top of feet brownish-green; rear of legs and base of feet yellowish-green.

Habitat and Distribution Crepuscular, frequenting swampy regions and stream margins in densely forested areas. A solitary nester building a flimsy platform of sticks, usually on a well foliated horizontal branch of a Japanese Cedar, at heights of 7–20 m. Possibly double brooded on occasions, eggs laid mid-May, also mid-July. Species thought to be confined to Japan where it breeds on the Izu-shoto Archipelago off Yokahama; also the Kanagawa and Shizuoka Prefectures on Honshu, the Yamanashi Prefecture north of Mount Fuji and Tokushima Prefecture at the eastern end of Shikoku Island.

White-backed Night Heron

Gorsachius leuconotus
(Nycticorax leuconotus)

Description Length 54 cm. Head and short nuchal crest black, with prominent white patch around eye. Chin white; neck and upper breast pale chestnut. Back, wings and tail dark chocolate brown, but with white dorsal patch, this often not apparent. Lower breast and rest of underparts whitish, mottled with fawn. Lores greenish-yellow. Iris dark brown (varies). Bill mainly black but yellowish towards base of lower mandible. Legs and feet yellowish (vary according to season). Sexes alike.

Habitat and Distribution A nocturnal species which frequents marshlands and dense forest. The nest is a platform of sticks built on branches, usually overhanging water. Restricted to Africa south of the Sahara, occurring from Senegal in the west to the Sudan, then south to the Okavango swamps of Botswana and Port Elizabeth. Most sightings are from north-east Zaire (upper tributaries of the Uele River) and Zambia (the Barotse Plain along the upper Zambezi).

White-backed Night Heron

White-eared Night Heron
(Magnificent Night Heron)

Gorsachius magnificus
(Nycticorax magnifica)

Description Length 54 cm. Crown, malar patch, nape, nuchal crest and hindneck blackish-brown. A broad white band extends backwards from eye, separating crown from malar patch. Throat and lower face white. Sides of neck broadly banded longitudinally with buffish-orange and blackish-brown. Back, wings and tail greyish-chocolate brown (tinged purple in male). Breast and underparts whitish, mottled with brown. Loral and orbital skin greenish-yellow. Iris yellow. Bill blackish, lower mandible tinged greenish-yellow. Legs and feet pale green. The female has duller head colours and shorter crest feathers.

Habitat and Distribution Frequents swampy, densely forested regions including bamboo zone. First seen on the island of Hainan off China's south-east coast in 1898. Distribution little known, with sightings from lower slopes of Wuchih Shan, near Ching-te in Anhwei province, Fu-chou and Chien-yang in Funkien, on the tributaries of the Min Chiang south-west of Fu-chou, and most recent new locality Tien-mu in Chekiang Province.

Tiger Bittern
(Malay Bittern or Malay Night-Heron)

Gorsachius melanolophus

Description Length 51 cm. Crown ashy black, as is the long bushy crest emanating from nape of neck. Rest of upperparts including back mainly reddish-brown, closely and finely barred transversely with black (hence the name Tiger Bittern). The greyish-black primaries and secondaries are tipped with reddish-brown and white. Tail black but tinged reddish at tip. Chin and throat white, foreneck and upper breast sandy pink, streaked with dark brown and black. Rest of underparts whitish, but heavily blotched and spotted with rufous and black on lower breast and abdomen. Iris golden yellow. Bill pinky yellow, but culmen and tip horny brown. Orbital skin greenish-grey, suffused with red when breeding. Legs and feet dull green, brownish in front. Sexes alike. The Nicobar Tiger Bittern (*G.m. minor*) is slightly smaller but of similar plumage and with the same behaviour, habitat, food and voice.

Characteristics and Behaviour
Closely related to the pond herons and the Night Heron (*Nycticorax nycticorax*); larger than the Cinnamon Bittern (*Ixobrychus cinnamomeus*) of which it is very reminiscent. Largely nocturnal, extremely shy and difficult to approach. Perhaps not as rare a species as is generally believed. Habits and behaviour similar to Night Heron. If disturbed flies a little way to a nearby tree, but is quick to move on again should an approach be attempted. The flight is noiseless and on quickly flapping wings.

Habitat Favours marshy areas and streams in the seclusion of dense forest.

Food Feeds in a typical heron-like fashion at waterholes and the edges of streams in thickly forested regions. Fish, frogs, lizards, molluscs and insects are all part of the diet.

Voice Usually a very silent bird. The only recorded notes are of a sitting bird, these include a short croak and a 'hissing' sound.

Display Not recorded.

Breeding Nests in thick forest regions. Nest is a flimsily constructed platform of twigs, which may or may not be lined, usually built close to a stream in a small overhanging tree at a height of between

5 and 8 m. Although the nests are in no way concealed, their position causes them to be overlooked. Only rarely breeds in reed beds. Eggs three to five, white and slightly tinged with blue. Size 46 × 37 mm. A very close sitter, remaining on the eggs until within touching distance. The incubation period is not known, nor is it known if the incubation, nest building or feeding of the young is shared by both sexes. The season in Assam is chiefly May and June; in south-west India end of May to August which coincides with the heaviest rains.

Distribution In India resident in the heavy rainfall areas of southern Western Ghats (Kerala); western Mysore (including the Nilgiri Hills), and north to 15°50′N; also Assam and Manipur. Also breeds Burma, Thailand, Indochina, south China, Taiwan, Borneo, Sumatra and Java. Winters in Sri Lanka from the foothills up to 1800 m, and south-west India up to 800 m. Arrives on the west coast of Sri Lanka during October and November. Little known about migration but birds have been observed in India during August, September and October flying in a southerly direction. *G.m. minor* breeds and apparently resident on Nicobar Islands but rare; has been reported at Katchel, Tillangchong and False Harbour. *G.m. hutteri* breeds Philippines. *G.m. rufolineatus* breeds Palawan Islands.

Tiger Bittern

60

New Guinea Tiger Heron
(Forest Bittern)

Zonerodius heliosylus

Description　Length 71 cm. The dark blackish-brown feathers of upperparts are tipped with buff or pinkish-buff, thus producing a transverse striping effect. Underparts whitish or buffish-white. Lores and orbital skin sulphur yellow. Iris yellow. Bill mainly ashy grey, but tinged with green in female. Legs lemon yellow. Sexes alike but in the female the lores and orbital skin are yellow, tinged with green.

Habitat and Distribution　Found along rivers, especially those flowing in heavy forest, being particularly fond of trees that overhang water. Does not frequent reed beds etc. Occurs in New Guinea, particularly in western Irian Jaya, and along the Mimika River. Breeding season variable.

White-crested Tiger Heron
(African Tiger Heron)

Tigriornis leucolophus
(Tigrisoma leucolophus)

Description　Length, standing 66–80 cm to top of head. Feathers of upperparts black, barred with warm buff. Male's white crest is partly hidden by black feathers of nape. Crown black. Bare facial skin green. Iris yellow. Bill, upper mandible dusky brown, lower yellowish-green. Legs brownish in front, yellowish to rear. In the female the barring of the feathers is much narrower, giving a much darker appearance.

Habitat and Distribution　Found in the equatorial rain forests of tropical Africa. Breeding May to July in the west, and from November to January in the east. Builds platform nest in tree.

Fasciated Tiger Heron

Tigrisoma fasciatum

Description　Length 66 cm, the smallest of the Tiger Herons. Head, sides and back of neck, back and wings blackish-brown, finely and closely barred transversely with buff, bolder on neck. Foreneck and breast white, streaked with dark brown. Flanks slaty grey; abdomen tawny. Orbital skin yellowish but varies in colour. Iris yellow. Bill dark brown above, greenish-yellow below, and a strip of feathers over base of lower mandible; whitish spot at tip of mandible. Legs dusky brown. *T.f. salmoni* is similar, but abdomen less tawny; wings and tail shorter. No mandibular feathering. *T.f. pallescens* is paler overall, especially so on abdomen; also slightly larger. No mandibular feathering.

Habitat and Distribution　Inhabits hilly country with fast-flowing streams. Nothing known of breeding activities. The nominate has been recorded from Rio de Janeiro and Rio Grande do Sul in south-east Brazil, and the Mato Grosso in the north-west. *T.f. salmoni* occurs in Costa Rica and Panama, Colombia, Venezuela, Ecuador and northern Peru. *T.f. bolivianus* occurs in southern Peru, Bolivia, north-west Argentina and at Bonplan in Misiones Province of Argentina.

Rufescent Tiger Heron
(Lineated Tiger Bittern)

Tigrisoma lineatum

Description　Length 70 cm. Head, sides and back of neck rich chestnut, very closely and finely barred with black on neck. Throat and foreneck whitish with long vertical streaks of brown and buff. Back, tail and wings very dark greeny brown, finely barred and streaked with black. Orbital skin yellow. Iris yellow. Bill dusky yellow above, fawny yellow below (variable). Legs dusky brown in front, greenish behind. Sexes similar (female possibly smaller). *T.l. marmoratum* is larger than the nominate.

Habitat and Distribution Favours the wooded margins of swamps. Occurs in Central America from the Honduras bank of the River Coco, bordering on Nicaragua, to Panama. But mainly in South America from Ecuador, the Upper Amazon, and the Guianas, south to Bolivia, Paraguay and Uruguay; also Trinidad. *T.l. marmoratum* prefers more hilly terrain and breeds in Paraguay, Argentina, Bolivia and the Mato Grosso of Brazil. It is a tree-nesting species, constructing a flimsy platform nest.

Bare-throated Tiger Heron
(Mexican Tiger Bittern)

Tigrisoma mexicanum

Description Length 71–81 cm, the largest of the tiger herons. Crown and nape black; sides of face slaty grey. Back and sides of neck buffy chestnut, closely barred with dark brown. Throat void of feathers, having greenish-yellow gular patch. Foreneck buffish-white, streaked with black; breast tinged cinnamon; belly deep cinnamon. Bare facial skin of

Bare-throated Tiger Heron

62

deeper green than gular patch. Iris yellow. Bill blackish. Legs dark green. *T.m. fremitus* is a little larger on average, and striped more boldly.

Habitat and Distribution Frequents mangrove swamps and saline or brackish waters; also inland areas. A tree-nesting species with nest platform usually overhanging water. Breeds along Pacific coast of Central America, also inland in north-west Colombia to the Rio Atrato valley. At the eastern end of its range it has been recorded at Guemez in Tamaulipas State, about 225 km from the Rio Grande. Also occurs in Yucatán, the eastern slopes of Honduras and south through Costa Rica and Panama. *T.m. fremitus* is possibly restricted to Mexico in the upland area that borders on the states of Sonora and Sinaloa at 440 m with neighbouring freshwater streams and rivers.

Zigzag Heron
Zebrilus undulatus

Description Length 30 cm. Crown, back, wings and tail blackish-brown; feathers of back and wings finely and closely barred with pale buff. Has short crest of blackish feathers. Head, neck and upper breast are mottled with greyish-buff and brown. Underparts buff, finely streaked and barred with brown. No bare facial skin. Iris yellow. Bill short, stoutish and pointed, dusky brown. Legs and feet greyish-black. Sexes alike. Immature birds are said to have bright rufous face, neck, breast and underparts.

Habitat and Distribution Frequents marshes, pools and rivers bordered with trees. Occurs in northern and central parts of South America, with records from coastal areas of the Guianas, also Venezuela (Orinoco delta), the basins of the Rio Negro and upper Orinoco, the land bordering Colombia, also Ecuador and north-east Peru, stretches of the Amazon in the east and as far as the western Mato Grosso (Brazil) near the Bolivian frontier.

Cinnamon Bittern
(Chestnut Bittern)

Ixobrychus cinnamomeus

Description Length 38 cm. Male: upperparts including bushy crest deep reddish-brown with chestnut wing quills. Chin and throat whitish; dark stripe down middle of foreneck. On each side of the upper breast is a small area of black and reddish-brown feathers with buff borders, which are almost hidden by the very long breast feathers. Rest of underparts pale cinnamon. Orbital skin deep rosy red. Iris yellow, orange or pink red. Bill greeny yellow or pale orange-yellow, base rosy red, culmen blackish. Female: upperparts chestnut; the black spots on scapulars and wing coverts bordered with buff. Crown blackish. Underparts buffish-chestnut, with a bold brown median streak down foreneck and breast; flanks marked with parallel lines of small brown dashes. Rest of underparts streaked with dark brown. Orbital skin yellowish.

Characteristics and Behaviour More slender and smaller than the pond herons. The sexes are distinguishable in flight by the undersides of the wings which are pale pinky chestnut in the male and reddish-brown in the female. Not a gregarious species, and active mainly in the hours of twilight. Usually only seen in broad daylight when flushed, but during the breeding season it is quite common to see one flying to or from a reed bed. In flight the neck is drawn in and the rounded wings have a very quick beat. Other aspects of behaviour much as for the pond herons and Chinese Little Bittern (*I. sinensis*).

Habitat Frequents flooded paddy fields, reed beds and swamps; less often tidal mangroves and coastal backwaters. Often in the company of the Chinese Little Bittern.

Food The diet includes fish, even up to 13 cm in length, also frogs, molluscs, and a variety of aquatic insects. Catches its prey by lungeing rapidly with head and bill, the rest of body remaining quite motionless.

Voice For the most part a silent bird, but come the breeding season it constantly utters 'kok-kok-kok-kok'. The courtship song consists of 'gook gook gook …' repeated eight times, the first five gradually increasing in volume, the remainder pitched a few tones lower.

Display When courting a female, the male flies slowly in front of her on stiffish, slowly beating wings, uttering 'ek-ck-ek-ek', finally perching on the uppermost branches of a low tree. The visual display not unlike that of the Short-eared Owl.

Breeding The nest is built in a reed bed or similar situation. A collection of reed stems and leaves is fashioned into a small pad, with flattened reed stems serving as a foundation, but kept well clear of the water and mud. The eggs number four to five (sometimes six), they are white, occasionally with a bluish tint, and almost cylindrically shaped. Size 36.5 × 26.4 mm. Nest building, incubation (period not known) and feeding of young (by regurgitation) shared by both sexes. Breeding occurs between June and September, as soon as the monsoon rains are well under way; this is generally July to August.

Distribution Breeds throughout Pakistan, India, Sri Lanka and the Andaman, Nicobar and Maldive Islands; the Indus Valley being the approximate western distribution limit. Also breeds in Burma, Thailand, Malaysia, the Philippines, Sunda Islands, the Celebes, China from Manchuria to Hainan, and the Ryukyu Islands.

Schrenck's Little Bittern
Ixobrychus eurhythmus

Description Length 36 cm. Male: upperparts mainly chestnut, darker on back; crown blackish-brown. Flight feathers dusky grey; median coverts rich buff; rest of wing mainly chestnut. Tail blackish-brown. Throat whitish, rest of underparts buffish. Iris yellow. Bill, upper mandible medium dusky brown, lower mandible greenish-yellow. Loral and orbital skin usually olive-green, sometimes tinged with pink. Legs and feet dull greenish-fawn. Female similar but flecked with white above; underparts yellowish-buff streaked with brown.

Characteristics and Behaviour Adult birds can be readily distinguished from the Cinnamon Bittern (*I. cinnamomeus*) and the Chinese Little Bittern (*I. sinensis*) by their less contrasting wing plumage: the Cinnamon's wings are tawny coloured whilst those of the Chinese Little Bittern are buff and black. Schrenck's also has a much darker coloured back. Another useful and distinctive feature is the pearly grey of the underwings which occurs in both sexes and at all ages.

Habitat Prefers low-lying areas, with swamps and wet grasslands. Likes to have dense vegetation into which it can retreat. However, it finds drier conditions and a lack of tree cover more acceptable than other small bitterns, with the possible exception of the Chinese Little Bittern.

Food Feeding techniques not recorded, but is known to feed principally on small fish with *Carassius auratus*, the Gold Fish, being the one most often taken. Also takes shrimps, isopods, dragonfly nymphs and other insect larvae.

Voice If flushed, utters a low pitched squawk. During the breeding season an oft-repeated 'gup-gup-gup'. Is said to be more vocal than either the Cinnamon or the Chinese Little Bittern.

Display Nothing recorded, but the male bird calls noisily during the period of courtship.

Breeding The principal season is during May and June, when a mound of grasses and dry reed stems is constructed on, or close to the ground under the cover of tall vegetation or shrubs; sometimes lined with a few leaves or a little clay thus reducing the effects of water seepage. Three to five white eggs are laid, measuring 32 × 20 mm. Incubation is shared by both birds and commences with the first egg, but duration is not on record. The female alone builds the nest, but the male plays the major role in feeding the chicks.

Distribution Breeding occurs south of latitude 52°N, from the lakes and valleys at the south-east of Lake Baikal, eastwards through central Amurland, Ussuriland to Sakhalin; south to Hokkaido and northern Honshu, also Sadoshima (off the north-west coast of Honshu). A rare summer visitor to Korea (with no proof of breeding). Breeds in China as far south as Shanghai, there are also records from Kwangtung, but it is uncertain just how far westwards it occurs in China. Winters in southern China, Taiwan, Indochina and Thailand. Also found in Malaya, Sumatra, Java, the Philippines (where it is far less common than the Chinese Little Bittern), and the Celebes.

Least Bittern
Ixobrychus exilis

Description Length 35.5 cm. Male: crown, back and tail glossy greenish-black. Face and neck rufous brown; throat whitish; breast fawnish-buff with a blackish patch on either side of the latter. Wing primaries slaty; greater coverts and inner secondaries rich chestnut; lesser and median coverts fawnish-buff, forming a conspicuous wing patch. There is a whitish stripe along each of the scapulars. Underparts fawnish-buff; underwings pale yellow. Lores vary from dull yellow to pale green. Iris yellow. Bill yellow, dusky at edge. Legs and feet greenish-yellow, often suffused with brown. Female: crown and mantle dark brownish-chestnut; two light stripes on scapulars; throat darkly streaked. In comparison with the nominate, *I.e. erythropus* is more rufous on the face and neck; *I.e. bogotensis* has more richly coloured underparts; *I.e. hesperis* is slightly larger; *I.e. pullus* is darker above with little contrast between coverts and flight feathers; *I.e. peruvianus* is less bright and larger.

Habitat and Distribution Similar to the Little Bittern (*I. minutus*) with which it could be confused. Prefers freshwater habitat amongst dense vegetation. Nest is a platform of reed stems or catstail, just above water level. Breeds in eastern and central North America, from parts of southern Canada to the Gulf of Mexico and the Caribbean, also eastern Mexico to El Salvador and Nicaragua. *I.e. erythropus* breeds from Panama Canal, north Colombia and Venezuela, south to Paraguay; *I.e. bogotensis* breeds Suba marshes, Bogotá, Colombia; *I.e. hesperis* breeds west of Rockies, Buena Vista Lake, Kern County, California; *I.e. pullus* breeds Tobari Bay, Sonora, Mexico; *I.e. peruvianus* breeds Vegueta, Lima, Peru. *I.e. limoncochae* occurs eastern Ecuador.

Streaked Bittern
(Stripe-backed Bittern)
Ixobrychus involucris

Description Length 33 cm. Plumage predominantly sandy buff, somewhat paler on underparts. Foreneck pale buff with vertical lines of brown streaking. Narrow black band on crown and nape. Back streaked with blackish and buff; tips of primaries rufous. Iris pale yellow. Bill yellowish-brown. Legs and feet greenish-yellow. Sexes alike.

Habitat and Distribution Frequents shallow marshes where it is a solitary breeder amongst the reeds and rushes, building a small platform of stems 30–60 cm above water. Breeding distribution in South America not fully known, but thought to extend from south-east Brazil, through Paraguay to northern Argentina and Chile to about 40°S; perhaps also to northern Patagonia. Season October and November.

Little Bittern

Ixobrychus minutus

Description Length 36 cm. Male: crown, nape, crest, back, scapulars, rump and tail black; many of the feathers on back broadly but faintly scalloped with grey. Innermost secondaries black. Sides of both head and neck greyish-pink. Throat and foreneck whitish or buff. Upper breast ochre with lanceolate feathers; lower breast dusky maroon. Flanks ochre with indistinct dusky shaft-lines. Rest of underparts white. The closed wing has a large patch of greyish-blue which all but hides the dusky dark brown flight feathers of the resting bird. Orbital skin pale liquid green. Iris pale yellow to orange-yellow. Bill yellow, creamy yellow, or purplish-yellow (red at base when breeding). Legs and feet greenish-yellow. In the female the areas on the upperparts which are black in the male are largely replaced with chestnut brown and buff. Shoulder patch of chestnut brown. Underparts chestnut and rufous, streaked with reddish-buff.

Characteristics and Behaviour Both a smaller and slimmer bird than the pond herons. A solitary species of crepuscular habits, usually seen during daytime only when flushed. Should an incubating bird be stumbled upon it will freeze into stillness, becoming almost invisible against the background of reeds. In flight the neck is drawn in, the wing

beat is quick and the striking contrast between pale wing coverts and dark body becomes apparent.

Habitat Backwater ponds with dense marginal vegetation, wooded swamps with reed beds, overgrown riverbanks, and similar well vegetated areas are most frequented.

Food Adopts a hunchback stance at the water's edge of a reed bed, poised to strike out with neck and bill at insects or other food items. Takes fish, frogs, molluscs, crustaceans, and many insects.

Voice The low croaking 'hogh' of the male is repeated at the rate of 25 to the minute, and this is often sustained over long periods at an amazingly regular tempo. Other notes, a frog-like croak, 'wuk'.

Display No record.

Breeding In late April birds begin to arrive on their European breeding grounds, but do not nest until much later, departing again by late September. A common species in the Kashmir Valley (India), where it breeds abundantly from May to July. Not a colonial nesting species. The nest is a bed of rushes constructed by bending down several reed stems and adding other items of vegetation to form a small platform or pad. Dense reed beds are usually chosen as nest sites; occasionally, untimely fluctuations in the water level will cause nests to become swamped with water. Eggs four to six (seven), white but sometimes tinged with pale blue. Size 34 × 26 mm. Laid at intervals of two days, incubation commencing with the first egg and continuing for 16–17 days. Nest building, incubation of eggs and feeding of young are shared by both sexes.

Distribution Breeds in central and southern Europe, Asia Minor, Israel, Iran, Turkestan, Afghanistan and western Siberia; wintering in Africa south to Cape Province. Also breeds Sind (Pakistan), Nepal, Uttar Pradesh, east to

Little Bittern (*Ixobrychus minutus*) ♂

Assam; normally in the lowlands, but in the Vale of Kashmir up to 1500–1800 m. Here it is mainly a resident bird making but local migratory movements. The Madagascar Little Bittern (*I.m. podiceps*), occurs from sea level to 1000 m in the Humid East, the Sambirano and the Western Savanna of Madagascar. *I.m. payesii* breeds from Senegal to Aden; migrates to Cape Province. *I.m. dubius* breeds east and south-west Australia. *I.m. novaehollandiae* breeds in New Zealand.

Chinese Little Bittern
(Yellow Bittern)
Ixobrychus sinensis

Description Length 38 cm. Male: back light brown to yellowish-brown. Chin, throat and front of neck pale yellow. Bushy crest and crown black; sides of head and rear of neck vinous pink. Wings blackish; rump dark grey; tail bluish-black. Upper breast pale yellowish, streaked with buff. Remaining underparts pale yellowish-buff. Bare facial skin pale greenish-yellow. Iris orange-yellow. Bill, lower mandible pale yellowish-pink, culmen horny brown. Bare facial skin pale greenish-yellow. Legs and feet either yellow or greenish-yellow. Female very similar but usually has a buff line running down centre of throat and foreneck.

Chinese Little Bittern

Characteristics and Behaviour A small slender bird, predominantly rufous, yellowish and brown. In flight the contrasting black wings and yellowish-brown body are a guide to its identity. As with several species of bittern it is mainly crepuscular or nocturnal by habit, becoming more active in daytime when cloudy or overcast. If taken by surprise, particularly when incubating, will freeze into position with neck upstretched and bill pointing skywards.

Habitat Often seen in company with the Cinnamon Bittern (*I. cinnamomeus*), both birds favouring the same bushy growth of inland swamps, flooded fields of standing rice, coastal mangroves and quiet backwaters.

Food Usually fish, frogs and molluscs; also insects, including flies. Acquired by rapid lunges of the neck and head.

Voice A very occasional 'kaka-kaka'.

Display Not on record.

Breeding Nest usually placed in a reed bed or in low shrubby growth at the edges of ponds, but clear of the water and mud, up to heights of about 1 m or so. The four to six very pale blue or green-blue eggs are laid just as soon as the monsoons have filled the swamps and hollows; usually June to September. Egg size 31 × 24 mm. Incubation shared by both sexes (exact period not known), and commences with the first egg. Eggs laid on consecutive days. Both birds also tend the young.

Distribution Throughout Pakistan and India, from the Indus valley eastwards to beyond Assam, from Nepal southwards to Kerala, Sri Lanka and the Andaman and Nicobar Islands. Also Burma, Thailand, Malaya, China, Japan, New Guinea and the Caroline Islands.

African Dwarf Bittern
Ixobrychus sturmii
(Ardeirallus sturmii)

Description Length 30 cm. Head, hindneck, back, wings and tail dark slaty black, with elongated plumes on head. Foreneck and breast pale buff but boldly marked with vertical rows of black blotches. Belly tawny buff with large blotches of black. Iris brownish-red. Bill blackish, lower mandible often dusky green (variable). Legs and feet greenish-yellow in front, yellow behind and beneath toes. Sexes alike but female has yellow iris.

Habitat and Distribution Said to favour the margins of freshwater ponds, rivers and streams with overhanging forest, in preference to marshland. A platform of twigs is usually built in a thorn bush, mimosa or some other tree overhanging water. Nests reported May/June in Kenya; February in the Transvaal; March in Zambia; September/October also October to December in Zimbabwe and South Africa. Probably breeds throughout most suitable areas of Africa south of the Sahara, from Senegal to the Sudan, and south to about East London in Cape Province.

American Bittern
Botaurus lentiginosus

Description Length 66 cm. Deep sandy brown above finely speckled with black. Flight feathers black. Crown rusty brown. Pale stripe runs from base of bill over, and extending beyond, eye. A narrow band of black runs a little way down side of neck from below eye. Throat whitish, shading to buffish on breast, the latter heavily streaked with rufous feathers edged with black. Belly pale rufous and streaked like breast. Bare lores greenish-yellow. Iris yellow. Bill dull yellow, upper mandible with dark tip. Legs and feet pea green. Sexes alike.

Habitat and Distribution Frequents marshland with tall dense growth. Constructs a platform nest of aquatic vegetation. A solitary nester; season mainly May to June. Breeds in North America as far north as British Columbia, Great Slave Lake (Mackenzie), Alberta, Saskatchewan and east to Hudson Bay, and from central Quebec to Newfoundland. Breeds as far south as Texas and Florida.

South American Bittern
(Pinnated Bittern)
Botaurus pinnatus

Description Length 75–76 cm. Rear and sides of neck closely barred brown and buff. Crown blackish. Yellow line over eye. Back and wings buff but heavily and very boldly barred and mottled with dark brown. Tail mainly slaty grey (in male). Throat whitish. Foreneck buffish, lightly streaked with brown. Breast and belly pale rufous, boldly streaked with dark rufous brown. Bare lores greenish-yellow. Iris pale yellow. The massive bill pale yellow, dusky on culmen and towards tip. Legs and feet yellowish-green. Sexes alike but female smaller. *B.p. caribaeus* has longer bill and generally paler upperparts, the ground colour being whitish rather than buffish. Has fewer streakings on throat.

Habitat and Distribution Frequents freshwater swamps with tall dense cover, in coastal areas or savannas inland. Nest typical of the genus. Season July to October in Trinidad; February to March in Brazil. Breeds tropical South America, from Colombia, Venezuela, the Guianas and Brazil, south to Ecuador, Uruguay and Argentina (to Buenos Aires). *B.p. caribaeus* breeds May and occurs in Central America.

Australian Bittern
(Brown Bittern)
Botaurus poiciloptilus

Description Length 100 cm. Crown, nape and lower face deep dusky brown. Upper face and stripe above eye rufous buff. Rear and sides of neck blackish-brown. Rest of upperparts blackish-brown and mottled with pinkish-buff. Foreneck pale buff with broad streaks of dark brown. Remaining underparts pale buff, mottled and closely barred with dark brown. Bare facial skin pale green. Iris yellow or reddish-yellow. Bill brownish above, yellowish below. Legs and feet dull yellowish-green. Sexes alike but female smaller.

Habitat and Distribution Dense reed beds and similar situations are the haunts of this bird. Nest typical of the genus. Breeds October to February, and is fairly common in Australia throughout New South Wales, except north-west tip; south-east regions of South Australia and Queensland; also south-west region of Western Australia. Throughout Tasmania, extending to New Zealand.

Eurasian Bittern

Botaurus stellaris

Description Length 76 cm. Upperparts golden brown, richly mottled and barred with black. Head and neck more uniform brown, with crown and nape black. Throat whitish, offset by a blackish moustachial streak below which it is light yellowish-buff, overlaid with stripes of reddish-brown and black. Feathers of foreneck thick and elongated. Bare loral region green to pale blue. Iris yellow. Bill greenish-yellow. Legs and feet pale green. Sexes alike.

Characteristics and Behaviour Flies slowly and reluctantly, low over the reeds, with retracted neck and trailing legs; the broad rounded wings are noticeably barred with reddish-brown and black. A solitary and crepuscular bird, spending the day skulking secretively amongst dense reed beds. It walks with bowed head and hunched up shoulders, and has a characteristic mannerism, when hiding, of 'freezing' in an elongated pose with its bill pointed vertically upwards, the plumage providing excellent camouflage.

Habitat A bird exclusively of lowland swamps and wetlands covered with dense vegetation, particularly fond of sheltered open waters with a heavy covering of reeds. Sometimes emerges onto the more open areas of lake shores and riverbanks.

Food Prey is stalked and siezed with powerful thrusts of its pointed bill. Food is searched for over a wide area and it is doubtful whether the common belief in its crepuscular habits is justified. It consumes a wide variety of food including small mammals, birds, reptiles, insects and fish. It is particularly fond of eels and is able to deal with them up to lengths of 30–40 cm.

Voice A harsh 'aark' is sometimes uttered, but its more usual call is a deep booming 'u-hump' which follows a series of taps and coughs as the bird inhales. The booming is usually given in four double notes and has great carrying power, up to 4 km.

Display Although little is known about the courtship activities of the Bittern, birds have been observed indulging in what can be described as territorial flights above the reed beds, erratic in nature, at heights of up to 60 m, and ranging over a square mile or so of the marshland.

Breeding Usually concealed in a dense reed bed, the nest is an assemblage of matted reeds and other marsh vegetation put together at random by the female alone, to form a pad that is soon flattened with use. Between April and May, four to five olive-brown, occasionally spotted, eggs are laid (as many as seven have been recorded). Size 53 × 39 mm. Incubation commences with the first egg and lasts for about 25 days, it is undertaken solely by the female as is the rearing and feeding of the young. Feeding is done by regurgitation. The male searches for food, but mostly he defends the breeding territory.

Distribution Breeding range extends over a wide area in Europe and Asia. In England it breeds from the Norfolk downs to Kent, and on the Royal Society for the Protection of Birds reserve at Leighton Moss in Lancashire. It stretches eastwards through southern Sweden,

70

Bittern (*Botaurus stellaris*)

southern Finland to Japan. Being only a partial migrant it will remain to winter in areas where the water does not freeze regularly. Populations from the western Palearctic migrate south to Africa, some even crossing the Sahara, and it has been recorded as far south as Zaire. Birds from the central and eastern Palearctic travel south and can be found in the northern half of the Indian subcontinent, Burma, and throughout central China to the coastlands of China. Although in the Far East birds tend to be more boldly barred, *B.s. capensis* is now the only recognised subspecies. It inhabits the marshlands in the eastern half of southern Africa, with its range extending from Zambia to the Cape Province. Rainfall and changes in temperature tend to govern any local migration.

71

Black Bittern

Dupetor flavicollis

(Ixobrychus flavicollis)

Description Length 58 cm. Male: upperparts including wings, tail, sides of head and crown slaty grey, sometimes darker and almost black. On either side of the neck is a bright buffish-yellow band (hence *flavicollis*). Dull white feathers of chin and throat have a dotted rufous line running down the middle. Front of neck a mixture of rufous, buff and dark greyish-black. The dark slaty feathers of upperparts are edged with buffish-white, producing what has been described as a scalloped effect. Remaining underparts bluish-grey to brownish-black, a few of the abdominal feathers with white margins. Iris golden brown to red. Bare facial skin purple. Bill reddish horny brown, becoming paler and yellowish at tip of upper mandible and the forward half of lower mandible. Legs and feet dark brown. In the female upperparts tend to be browner and less slaty grey. Breast feathers streaked white and chestnut. Belly paler brown with more white central feathers.

Characteristics and Behaviour A solitary species, similar in general to the pond herons. A mainly black and reddish-buff bird with a most conspicuous light patch of white and buff extending from throat to side of neck. For the most part crepuscular and nocturnal by nature, skulking around in reed beds and swampy thickets by day, and only to be seen if flushed from these secluded quarters. As with other species of bittern, has the ability to freeze into stillness should it be suddenly confronted (especially when incubating). The camouflage of its plumage against a background of reed stems is most effective. The flight is similar to that of other small herons.

Habitat Does not seem to occur in tidal mangroves, but frequents low-lying marshy areas and swampy reed beds. Even, if conditions are suitable, up to 1200 m.

Food Fish, frogs, molluscs and insects; probably caught in a manner similar to that of the Chinese Little Bittern (*Ixobrychus sinensis*) and Cinnamon Bittern (*I. cinnamomeus*).

Voice A loud booming has been recorded during the breeding season.

Display Not known.

Breeding Season chiefly June to September, with local variations depending on adequate falls of rain to produce the required conditions. The nest is a platform of twigs and/or aquatic vegetation, with a central depression to receive the eggs, and is built in a reed bed or other suitable site. Four eggs are laid, which are white, tinged very lightly with pale blue or sea green. Size 42 × 31 mm. Incubation commences with the first egg and is shared by both sexes (period not recorded). Chicks are fed by regurgitation, both adults participating.

Distribution Thinly distributed throughout the adequately watered regions of Pakistan and north India. Quite common in south-west India (Mysore, Kerala) where the heavier rainfalls occur, and Sri Lanka. Also breeds in Burma, Thailand, Malaysia, Indochina, central and southern China, Greater Sunda Islands and the Celebes. Not recorded from the Andaman and Nicobar Islands. *D.f. australis* breeds Timor Island. *D.f. nesophilus* New Britain and New Ireland. *D.f. woodfordi* Solomon Islands. *D.f. gouldi* Moluccas, New Guinea and Australia. *D.f. pallidior* Rennell Island.

Family—Balaenicipitidae

Whale-headed Stork
(1 species recorded)

Whale-headed Stork
(Shoebill)

Balaeniceps rex

Description Length 115–130 cm. Plumage predominantly grey, the back having a greenish cast. Chest marked with black central plumes. Bill characteristically shoe-shaped being as broad as it is long, and dark grey in colour. Legs and feet darkish. Sexes alike.

Habitat and Distribution Particularly fond of large expanses of papyrus swamp, but also frequents open flood plains and the marshy borders of lakes and rivers. The nest is placed in high grass on dry land and consists simply of trampled and flattened down vegetation. One or two dull chalky-white eggs are laid. The breeding season varies, on the River Nile it has been recorded from December to March, and on Lake Kioga in Uganda from March to June. In Africa its general range extends from the Sudan, Uganda and Zaire as far south as the Katanga District.

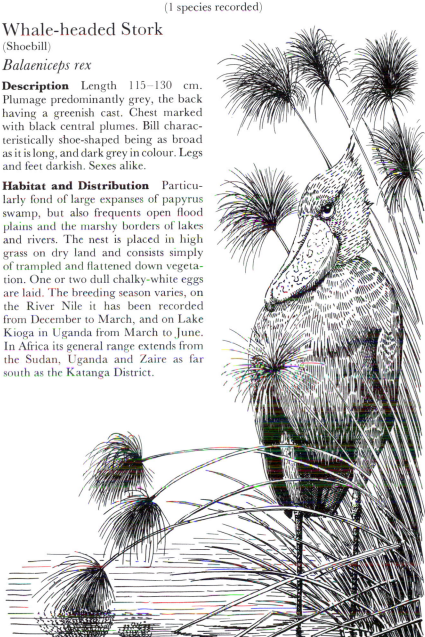

Family—Scopidae

Hammerhead Stork
(1 species recorded)

Hammerhead Stork
(Hammerkop or Hammerhead)

Scopus umbretta

Description Length 56–61 cm. An overall brown bird showing faint traces of purplish gloss on the back. It superficially resembles a small ibis or stork, but is easily identified by a pointed crest at the rear of the head which, when coupled with its large bill, gives the impression of a hammer-shape from whence its name is derived. Bill black, broad and flattened. Legs and feet blackish. Sexes alike but female usually smaller.

Characteristics and Behaviour A common and characteristic bird of Africa. Usually solitary, and with the peculiar habit of sitting crossways on tree branches, with folded legs. In flight the neck is carried partly retracted, and its broad rounded wings give the bird an owl-like appearance; the flight is low, with short sharp beats of the wing. It shares characteristics of both herons and storks. The Hammerhead, which is semi-nocturnal, lies at the centre of more native legends than any other species.

Habitat Frequents numerous waterside areas, from small streams at 2450 m to big rivers and large lakes. They are never very far away from trees, in which they roost, breed and seek refuge.

Food Walks and wades with a deliberate shuffle, disturbing prey such as insects, shrimps, small fishes, tadpoles and frogs with its feet. Forages for food both day and night.

Voice Although silent for the most part, it does have a sharp and shrill 'sikwee-sikwee-kwee-kwee', as well as the occasional grunt, and a low guttural 'kar-kar'. During the mating season it utters a sort of yapping cackle.

Display False mounting is the Hammerhead's most characteristic ritual and a somewhat bizarre display. Dancing ceremonies are also performed, accompanied by the 'yapping cackle'. Nuptial display flights also take place, accompanied by the occasional monotonous croaking.

Breeding Sticks, reed stems and any other rubbish that might be available, all go into the nest construction which is an enormous structure often 12–15 m above the ground in the fork of a tree. The nest is actually inside the structure and roofed over in the manner employed by a Magpie (*Pica pica*), but with a mud-lined entrance hole just large enough to permit the bird to squeeze inside. The nest is built over a period of two to four months, and the three to six dull white eggs are laid on a lining of waterweed and dry grass. Egg size 45 × 35 mm. Incubation continues for about 30 days and is shared by both birds. Nest may also be constructed amongst rocks, on the ground, or on a hill slope. Over its entire range the Hammerhead breeds in every month of the year.

Distribution The nominate breeds in Africa from Senegal to Nigeria. *S.u. minor* breeds in coastal regions from Sierra Leone to Nigeria. *S.u. bannermanni* breeds Cameroon to Aden and Cape Province, probably Madagascar.

Hammerhead Stork (*Scopus umbretta*)

Family—Ciconiidae

Storks
(17 species recorded)

Yellow-billed Stork
(Wood Ibis)

Ibis ibis
(Mycteria ibis)

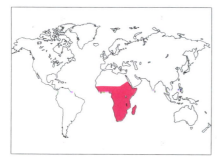

Description Length 95–105 cm. Predominantly dull white, but when breeding the feathers of back, scapulars, upper wing coverts and axillaries are tinged with crimson. The black primaries, secondaries and tail feathers have a purple and greenish gloss. Bare facial skin red to reddish-orange. Iris brown. Bill long, yellow, tipped with orange and slightly decurved. Legs, tibia pale orangey red, tarsus greyish-pink, toes black. Sexes alike.

Characteristics and Behaviour On ground the only possible confusion could be with the White Stork (*Ciconia ciconia*) which has a straight red bill, white face feathers and red legs. In flight, when high overhead, the black tail distinguishes it from White Stork, White Pelican and Egyptian Vulture, all of which have white tails. A gregarious species that freely associates with heron species. Seldom very far from water, and spending much of its time standing or wading in the shallows, or resting on nearby sandbars or mudflats. Usually seen in low flight when travelling short distances, resorting to higher flight for longer journeys.

Habitat Equally at home in the saline waters of coastal lagoons, saltflats and beaches, or broad, shallow freshwater rivers with sandbanks, flooded meadows, waterholes and the shores of inland lakes.

Food Frogs, crustaceans and small fish are included in the diet. Prey is taken by submerging bill and head whilst wading in shallow water. Insects may also be taken.

Voice Bill clapping and a variety of harsh guttural sounds when at the nest. Otherwise a mainly silent bird.

Display Not recorded.

Breeding Season extends from September through March in the northern tropics (the dry season). June to September in Chad, here it is partially migratory between latitudes 12°N and 14°N. A colonial nester, building a platform of sticks in trees, bushes or on cliff ledges. A sparse lining of grass is added before the two to three dullish or greenish-white eggs are laid. Average size about 63 × 45 mm. Breeding season varies throughout its range, January to February in Gambia; November to February in Ghana; September to January in Nigeria; October in French Equatorial Africa; October to December in southern Sudan; June in Uganda; May in Kenya and on Tana River; August to September in Central Island and Lake Rudolph; September in Malawi; June and July in Zambia.

Distribution Breeds south of the Sahara in Africa, from Gambia east to the Sudan, and on south to South Africa; also Madagascar. Thought to move to higher latitudes (but keeping on own side of equator) for moulting purposes. In Nigeria breeding birds are resident in northern savanna. From November to March (dry season) non-breeders are

Yellow-billed Stork (*Ibis ibis*) left.
African Spoonbill (*Platalea alba*) right.

commonly seen on the coast and along the large rivers, but these leave the humid regions for more northerly climes at the onset of heavy rains.

Milky Stork
Ibis cinereus
(Mycteria cinerea)

Description Length 97 cm. Plumage predominantly white, with black flight feathers. Bill long, tapering, somewhat decurved and rounded at the tip. During the breeding season the bill, which is tipped with white, becomes a brighter yellow, the facial skin becomes a more prominent red and the legs turn from grey to dark red. Sexes alike.

Habitat and Distribution Favours marshes, lakes, coastal areas, mudflats and mangroves. It breeds and is resident in South-East Asia, particularly in the lowlands of Malaya, Kampuchea and Cochinchina. Also breeds in Sumatra and Java.

Painted Stork

Ibis leucocephalus
(Mycteria leucocephalus)

Description Length 93 cm. An egret-like bird with long neck and legs. Head and neck white. Rest of upperparts also white but with close bars of glossy greenish-black. Black band across breast, and an area of pale rosy pink close to tail. Black quills on wings and tail. Underparts white. Bill orange-yellow, shading darker towards the greyish base. Legs and feet brown or pinkish-brown, at times almost red. Naked skin of face waxy yellow. Sexes alike.

Characteristics and Behaviour In flight the head is held lower than the rather hunched back, and the neck is outstretched. Out of breeding season usually seen singly, in pairs or small parties, but several thousands of birds may congregate in the larger heronries when nesting. After spells of feeding, they seem to spend much time soaring and circling in heat thermals, often in company with pelicans; or standing hunchbacked by the bank of a pond or stream.

Habitat Favours flooded fields, inland marshes and the banks of streams and rivers.

Food Usually hunts for food singly and may be seen wading slowly in the shallows with neck bent low and the large, partly open mandibles searching for food in the muddy bed. At times one leg will be seen to stir up the mud in what seems to be a deliberate attempt to disturb any fish that might otherwise remain motionless. At times of monsoon floods, when large numbers of fish have been washed down, the Painted Storks do feed gregariously, taking full advantage of such an abundant supply of food. The prey is mainly fish but such items as frogs, reptiles, crustaceans and insects all help to supplement the diet.

Voice Apart from bill clapping, a seemingly quiet bird. A low moan-like sound is produced when birds greet each other at the nest.

Display During greetings at the nest the oncoming bird will stretch forward with arched neck and bill held partly open, the sitting bird reciprocates in a similar manner and the low moan-like sound is uttered. Occasionally the arched necks are crossed. Bill clapping and bill touching is the greeting given by the sitting bird should its mate bring additional building material to the nest.

Breeding A colonial breeder, with mixed colonies often containing several thousand pairs. The nest is a large platform of twigs, sparsely lined with leaves and straw, additional material being added during occupation, such as leafy twigs, and for no apparent reason. Medium to large trees close to water house the nests, and it is not unusual to find about twenty built in a single tree. The three to four eggs are of a dull tarnished white, occasionally spotted or streaked with brown but very sparsely. Size 69.5 × 49 mm. Both sexes share the incubation (period undetermined) and care of the young. Breeding period is variable and coincides with the monsoon rains; in years of drought breeding may not occur. Usually August to October in north India; November to March further south; and March to April in Sri Lanka.

Distribution Breeds and is resident throughout the plains of Pakistan and

Painted Stork (*Ibis leucocephalus*)

India, also Sri Lanka, moving locally as water conditions demand. Also breeds in Burma, Thailand, Indochina, and south-west China. A vagrant to northern Malaya.

Wood Stork
(Wood Ibis)
Mycteria americana

Description Length 89–114 cm. Body plumage white except for black tail and flight feathers. Bare head and neck black. Bill blackish, long, stout, cone-shaped and decurved. Legs black, feet pinkish. Sexes alike.

Habitat and Distribution Chiefly inhabits areas of freshwater and wooded swamps. Great expanses of its favoured habitat, however, are being destroyed by droughts and drainage. Resident throughout its breeding range which includes most of peninsular Florida, Cuba, Dominican Republic, the southern tip of the Mexican plateau, along the coast of Mexico from Sinaloa and Veracruz southward, coastal Central America, northern Colombia, south-east Ecuador, and from north-eastern Venezuela, Guyana and north Brazil to the east coast of Argentina.

African Open-billed Stork

Anastomus lamelligerus

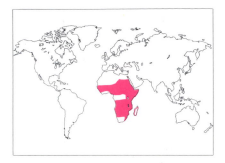

Description Length 92 cm. Adults uniformly brownish-black with the tips of feather shafts on the back, wing coverts and breast, flattened and broadened giving a sequin appearance. During the breeding season these feathers exhibit a sheen of greenish-bronze. Iris dull yellow. Bill large and heavy, dusky, with base of upper mandible greyish-yellow; when closed there is a wide gap along part of its length towards the tip. Legs and feet blackish. Sexes alike.

Characteristics and Behaviour Generally occurs in pairs or parties. It has a soaring flight during which it displays a characteristic broad, rounded tail and trailing legs. Partially nocturnal.

Habitat An aquatic species frequenting the grassy and marshy fringes of rivers and lakes, occasionally being found in clearings and on coastal lagoons.

Food Feeds mainly on freshwater mussels and other small aquatic animals. Small mussels are opened, washed and eaten underwater; larger ones are carried on to the bank and left to open, the birds returning, not necessarily to their own mussels but to whatever is available.

Voice Apparently completely silent.

Display No information.

Breeding Breeds in large colonies, the nest being a structure of sticks lined with grass, moss and reed stems, and built in reed beds or low trees, especially on islands in lakes. Two to three dull greyish-white eggs are laid, which on average measure 56 × 41 mm. The breeding season usually commences in February or March, although colonies have been observed where laying started in September and continued through to June and July.

Distribution Breeding range in Africa extends from Senegal and the Sudan to Angola and the Zambezi River, except in the forested area of West Africa. It is a straggler south of the Zambezi. *A.l. madagascariensis* occurs in Madagascar.

Asian Open-billed Stork

Anastomus oscitans

Description Length 81 cm. Standing 76 cm to top of head. During breeding season a white bird with a black rear portion. Flight feathers, scapulars and tail black with a purplish or greenish sheen. Bill, although pointed, looks blunter and less tapering than other storks, because of open space between dull greeny-fawn upper and slightly pinker lower mandible. Orbital skin and naked lores black. Iris dull white, grey or pale brown. Legs and feet dull pink. Out of breeding season the white parts are pale smokey grey. Sexes alike.

Characteristics and Behaviour May be mistaken at distance for a White Stork (*Ciconia ciconia*). The gap between the mandibles is a diagnostic feature. Large numbers congregate when nesting, at other times they occur singly or in small parties. On clear sunny days spends hour after hour circling high overhead, making its steep descent back to earth on wings half pulled in, with neck erect and legs dangling, banking, side-slipping and often turning quite violently before lightly touching down.

Habitat   Frequents inland waters and marshes, but very seldom riverbanks or out on tidal mudflats.

Food   The peculiarly shaped bill seems to serve as a tool for extracting the soft body content of a snail from its shell. The snail is held securely by the stork's feet whilst the operculum is cleanly and rapidly cut off. The bill tip is then inserted and the animal extracted. Often the operation is undertaken with the bill and head immersed in the water to well over the eyes. Molluscs form the bulk of its diet, especially the large snail, *Pila globosa*. Also takes crabs, frogs and other small animals that frequent its marshy feeding grounds.

Voice   During greeting ceremonies at the nest, bill clapping and the odd deep moaning sound. Otherwise a very quiet species.

Display   Not on record.

Breeding   A colonial nester, sometimes several thousand pairs breeding in mixed heronries along with darters, cormorants and egrets etc. A large round platform of twigs, with a lining of leaves in the nest depression, is constructed in a suitable tree, usually one partly submerged in water-filled depression. On occasions thirty or more nests are seen in one tree. Usually two to four white eggs are laid which soon become soiled. Size 58 × 41 mm. Incubated by both sexes for about 24–25 days. Young fed by regurgitation, a duty shared by both adults. In Pakistan and north India breeding season July to September; in more southerly parts of India, November to March; and in Sri Lanka, December to April. The exact time being determined by water conditions.

Distribution   Breeds and is resident throughout Pakistan, India and Sri Lanka, making local movements corresponding with availability of water. Also breeds in Burma, Thailand and eastwards to Indochina.

African Open-billed Stork (*Anastomus lamelligerus*)

White-bellied Stork
(Abdim's Stork)
Ciconia abdimii

Description   Length 76 cm. Contrasting plumage with most of upperparts, head, neck and breast glossy black with sheens of violet and green. Belly pure white, and a characteristic and conspicuous white rump. Bare facial skin of cheeks grey; that around eyes and on throat crimson. Bill green. Legs olive-green; toes and joints crimson.

Habitat and Distribution   Fond of cultivated areas or open dry ground. During the wet season resides in the drier savanna. Nest is a platform of sticks with grass lining, in which two to four chalky-white eggs are laid. Breeds during the rainy season and is widely distributed in West Africa from Senegal to Chad and the Central African Republic, eastwards to Ethiopia. Also in Tanzania as far south as 10°S. The non-breeding season is spent south of the Equator.

81

White Stork

Ciconia ciconia

Description Length 101 cm. Standing 106 cm to top of head. Except for the black wing quills and the longer scapulars, this is an entirely white bird, with long lanceolate feathers on head, neck and breast. Neck long. Legs long and bright red. The bare loral and orbital skin is black as is the chin. Iris brown or greyish-brown. Bill bright red. Sexes alike. The Asian White Stork (*C.c. asiatica*) is supposedly a little larger but may not be a valid subspecies. The Eastern White Stork (*C.c. boyciana*) is slightly larger. Black bill which is tinged purple at the base, is also larger. Iris rosy. Naked skin around eye and on throat red.

Characteristics and Behaviour In flight, the long neck is carried in an extended position, thereby readily distinguishing the White Stork from herons, pelicans and the Egyptian Vulture. Quite wary and difficult to approach when on its winter quarters in India, and yet seems almost domesticated when met with in most countries when nesting, being regarded as a harbinger of good luck. The flight consists of a few wing flaps and then a glide, speeds of 77 km/h being achieved in this deceivingly leisurely fashion. Commonly seen soaring, circling and gliding high overhead, making full use of the rising heat thermals. In *C.c. boyciana* the black bill is diagnostic.

Habitat Water meadows, marshy areas and grassy plains.

Food Frogs form one of its staple food items and it is said that they are attracted by the stork's bright red legs. Also included in the diet are reptiles, crustaceans, young rodents and occasionally fish. Also very large insects such as grasshoppers and locusts which are eaten from the egg stage through to the perfect insect. Because of its liking for locusts it has gained protection throughout much of its range.

Voice Bill clapping and the occasional hissing sounds, or cough-like noises, during the breeding season. Otherwise a very quiet bird.

Display During display, with the throat pouches puffed out to act as resonators, the mandibles are clapped or rattled very quickly, producing a castanet-like effect. The head is bent quickly backwards until the crown and culmen are almost in contact with the back, and then returned slowly to normal and beyond, the bill almost making contact with the ground. Often during courtship both birds will stand with breasts touching and mandibles clapping.

Breeding The nest is a large platform of sticks and twigs, placed on roof tops, chimney stacks, tall trees, cliffs and hay stacks. Old mosques are commonly utilised in the Middle East countries. During March and May three to five pure white eggs are laid. Size 73 × 59 mm. Incubation continues for about 30 days and the young leave the nest after 8–10 weeks.

Distribution Breeds up to 60°N in Europe, also in North Africa, and in western Asia eastwards and south of the Caspian Sea to north of the Persian Gulf. European birds winter mainly in Africa, migrating via Gibraltar or the Bosphorus; a few winter in Pakistan and northwest India (along with the Asiatic race),

White Stork (*Ciconia ciconia*)

arriving September/October. There are two sub-species. *C.c. asiaticus* breeds in Turkestan; most birds migrating south- wards to winter in Pakistan and north- west India. *C.c. boyciana* breeds from the Lower Ussuri and Amur Rivers to China, Korea and Japan and it winters in the Indian sub-continent.

White-necked Stork

(Woolly-necked Stork or Bishop Stork)

Ciconia episcopus

Description Standing 106 cm to top of head. White neck and black crown are very conspicuous. Apart from the elongated white tail coverts the rest of the plumage is black, sheened with purples and greenish-blues. Iris brown. Naked skin of face, chin and throat slaty black. Bill stout, long and tapering to a point, mainly black but red on culmen, along margins and at tip. Legs and feet red. Sexes alike. *C.e. stormii* is smaller, has a red bill and red facial skin (duller out of breeding season) and the black of the foreneck extends at least half way to bill.

Characteristics and Behaviour The white neck, black crown and long red legs are diagnostic of the species. May be met with in small parties, in pairs or singly, stalking about on both dry and marshy land. On sunny days habitually soars high on thermals, gliding and circling in mixed company along with vultures and other species of stork. At night-time selects tall trees in which to roost.

Habitat Favours flooded grasslands, ploughed fields when irrigated, marshy areas, and the banks of streams. Rarely frequents tidal creeks, and even then only well inland from the sea.

Food Stalks its prey on both dry and marshy land, where it catches large insects, reptiles, frogs, crabs, molluscs and fish. Seldom wades in water or immerses the bill, the fish in its diet being those left high and dry by receding flood waters or trapped in drying-up pools and waterholes. On occasion has been seen to fly in and out of a rising termite swarm eagerly snapping them up.

Voice Except for bill clapping (when the neck is bent over backwards until the crown rests between shoulder blades) and guttural noises a mostly silent bird.

Display Not recorded.

Breeding Not a colonial nester. An enormous platform of twigs and sticks up to 1 m across is constructed in a tall or medium-sized tree, at heights of up to 20 or 30 m. The deep depression is lined with straw and a sitting bird is almost hidden in its depths. If undisturbed the same site is often used in following years. Eggs three to four, white but during incubation become stained brown with mud due to contact with the birds' feet. Size 63 × 47 mm. Incubation period not known but is probably undertaken by both sexes, as is nest building and feeding of young (by regurgitation). Breeding season is variable. Pakistan and north India, July to September; southern India, December to March; Sri Lanka, January to April.

Distribution Resident and thinly distributed throughout the wetter parts of Pakistan and India. Up to 1250 m in Nepal. Also Sri Lanka and Burma. Locally common in low country and plateaux. *C.e. stormii* breeds in Borneo and rarely in Malaya. *C.e. neglecta* breeds from Malaysia to the Philippines and Sunda Islands. *C.e. microscelis* breeds in Africa from Senegal to Sudan and Cape Province.

White-necked Stork (*Ciconia episcopus*)

Black Stork
Ciconia nigra

Description Length 96 cm. Standing 106 cm to top of head. Upperparts including head and neck entirely black, the head with metallic sheen of green purple and bronze. Underparts, including lower breast, white. Iris either brown or black. Bare facial skin deep red. Bill red, paling at tip. Legs and feet scarlet red to coral. Sexes alike.

Characteristics and Behaviour In general appearance black above and white below. Very similar in behaviour to the White Stork (*C. ciconia*), but a more wary bird and one which is seen less frequently on the drier ground. Less gregarious than the White Stork, being met with in pairs or parties of up to 10 or 12; often seen in association with the White-necked Stork. In flight the wing beat tends to be faster than that of the White Stork, but with the neck extended in a similar manner. Makes less use of heat thermals for soaring than the White Stork.

Habitat When breeding chooses woodlands and cliff ledges. At other times frequents marshy areas, margins of lakes and ponds, also along riverbanks.

Food Shows a preference for fish when available, taking perch, rudd and roach. May be seen foraging in shallow woodland pools but seems to avoid the deeper waters. Will also take small eels, stickle-backs, newts, frogs and tadpoles, occasionally lizards and snakes. Other items in its diet are worms, insects and young rodents.

Voice Seems to be more vocal than the White Stork during breeding season, with a wider variety of guttural sounds. Most commonly heard sound at the nest is a soft 'chee lee' or 'chi chu', when the male arrives to relieve the female. Bill clapping not so regularly practised as with the White.

Display When greeting each other the birds display their white undertail coverts whilst moving the neck up and down or from side to side. Are also seen to walk around each other with tails spread and bills held in closely to the neck. When in an aggressive mood, again the undertail coverts are spread widely and with neck feathers erected, the bill is pointed upwards or swung in a side to side manner.

Breeding A large platform of sticks and twigs is built high in a tree, 10–25 m above ground, or perhaps on a rocky cliff but never, apparently, on buildings. The three to five oval eggs are white or blue-white, average size 65 × 49 mm. These are laid at intervals of two days, incubation commencing with the first or second egg. Both sexes share the incubation which varies from 32 to 46 days. The young fledge at between 63 and 71 days.

Distribution Last known breeding years for Denmark and southern Sweden are 1951 and 1953 respectively. Breeds sparingly in West Germany, Poland and east through Russia and Asia to northern China. Also breeds South Africa. Winters in Africa, Pakistan and northern India.

Black Stork (*Ciconia nigra*)

86

Maguari Stork
Euxenura maguari
(Ciconia maguari)

Description Length 100 cm. Plumage essentially white with contrasting black wings and tail. Facial region reddish-orange. Bill, legs and feet also reddish-orange.

Habitat and Distribution Inhabits lowland areas near sea level where it frequents expanses of marshy ground, and savanna ponds. The nest is a large structure of twigs built in low trees and bushes, often in close proximity to heronries. The breeding range lies in Guyana, Surinam, northern and south-eastern Venezuela, eastern Colombia, Brazil, Uruguay, Paraguay, northern Argentina southwards to Chubut. An occasional visitor to Chile.

Black-necked Stork

Xenorhynchus asiaticus
(Ephippiorhynchus asiaticus)

Description   Length 130 cm. Standing 135 cm to top of head. Back pure white from interscapulars to uppertail coverts. Underparts white from upper breast to undertail coverts. Rest of plumage black but with bright metallic sheens of greenish-blue, bronze and purple. Bill long and black, tip curving gently upwards. Naked skin of eyelids and throat pouch dull purple. Iris brown. Legs and feet coral red. Sexes alike but in the female the iris is bright lemon yellow.

Characteristics and Behaviour   A large white bird with black head and neck, long coral red legs and immense black bill. When flying overhead is seen to have a broad black band running diagonally across each wing (a diagnostic feature). By nature a shy and wary bird which may be met with either singly or in pairs, at no time gregarious. Like the White Stork (*Ciconia ciconia*), it utilizes heat thermals in its soaring flight and can be seen circling high overhead during the hotter parts of day.

Habitat   Frequents the margins of large rivers, lowland marshes and other boggy regions. On occasions visits tidal mangrove swamps.

Food   Has favourite feeding areas, usually in a very marshy area, or may be seen wading in the shallows. Sometimes assumes a squat position on the land at the edge of water. Principal food is fish, but will also take frogs, crabs, reptiles, or small rodents that chance by.

Voice   Apart from bill clapping, no other sound has been recorded of the adult bird. However, a sound described as 'chack wee wee wee' is produced by the downy young.

Display   Pairs have been seen to walk solemnly towards each other and, at a distance of 60 to 90 cm, extend the neck, outstretch and vigorously flutter their long wings until the tips brush against those of their partner, with both birds participating in rapid bill clapping.

Breeding   The nest is a massive structure of sticks and twigs forming a platform 1–2 m in diameter. A lining of straw and leaves is added to receive the eggs. Not a colonial nester, the single nest being 20–25 m high in the top of a tall solitary tree, often a Peepul (*Ficus religiosa*). Close proximity to water is not a necessity. The three to four oval white eggs measure 72 × 53 mm. Incubation period not on record. Both sexes help in nest building and feeding the young (by regurgitation).

Distribution   A resident bird with widespread distribution but nowhere plentiful. Breeds throughout Pakistan, India (rare in the south), Nepal and Sri Lanka. Also Burma, Malaysia, Thailand and Indochina. The race *X.a. australis* extends the species to Australia and possibly New Guinea.

Maguari Stork

Saddlebill Stork
Ephippiorhynchus senegalensis

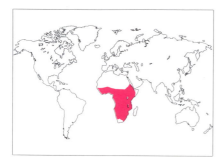

Description Length 145 cm. Head, neck, upper and underwing coverts and scapulars black. Tail black, with a blue and green iridescence during the breeding season display. Remainder of plumage, including the secondaries and primaries, white. Purplish stripe on bend of wing; bare crimson spot on breast. Iris brown. Bill large and red, characteristic in its black band and yellow frontal saddle. Legs dusky green with red knee joints; feet reddish. Sexes alike but iris yellow in female. Immature birds differ only in having dull grey instead of black markings.

Characteristics and Behaviour During its ponderous flight it displays diagnostic white primaries, and the legs trail beyond the tail. Normally a shy and solitary bird, but in certain areas they can become tame and approachable.

Habitat Frequents swamps and large rivers, also favours extensive flooded plains and lagoons.

Food Feeding behaviour similar to that of a heron, with slow stalking movements and fast jabs at its prey. Its diet consists mainly of insects, especially locusts, and it is protected in many regions for that reason. Also takes molluscs, frogs and lizards, and probes mud for lungfish.

Voice Usually a silent bird except for a rather feeble 'peep peep peep', but engages in bill clapping at the nest.

Display Courtship rituals include bill clapping ceremonies.

Breeding A solitary breeder, the nest being a large flat construction of sticks placed in tree tops, and possibly on cliffs. A single dull white egg, covered in minute pores, is laid between January and August. Average size 78 × 57 mm.

Distribution Breeds generally in Africa with its range extending from Senegal and the Sudan to South Africa, except for Somalia; a straggler south of the Orange River.

Jabiru
Jabiru mycteria

Description Length 130 cm. Plumage predominantly buffy white with the exception of head and neck which are a bare dusky black with a wrinkled texture. Characteristic red band around base of neck. Bill massive and dark grey, lower mandible sloping upwards at the tip. Iris appears to be black. Legs and feet black. In point of fact it is the largest flying bird in the New World.

Habitat and Distribution Frequents the marshy borders of streams and rivers, and other open marshy terrain. Nest is usually situated in the top of a palm tree. Breeds in the Guianas, Venezuela, Colombia, eastern Peru, Brazil, Paraguay, Uruguay and northern Argentina.

Saddlebill Stork (*Ephippiorhynchus senegalensis*)

Marabou

Leptoptilus crumeniferus

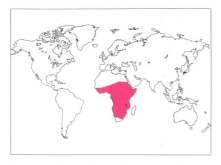

Description Length 115–130 cm. Naked skin of head dull red, spotted with black. Forehead blackish; hindneck red, tinged with blue; sides of neck and gular pouch fawnish-pink. Fluffy white collar around lower neck; upper back white. Rest of upperparts slaty grey; tail and flight feathers blackish. Breast and underparts white; long fluffy under tail coverts in breeding birds; underwing dark. Bill enormous, broad and dull yellowish-white at base, becoming white towards pointed tip. Iris dark. Legs blackish but often stained greyish by excreta. Sexes alike.

Characteristics and Behaviour This large bulky stork is unlikely to be confused with any other species in flight or on the ground. The Black Stork (*Ciconia nigra*) is much more slender, has a long neck and the black and white plumage is more contrasting. Vultures do not have so massive a bill and pelicans have whiter underwings. Walks with a hunched posture, head drawn into shoulders, with partly inflated gular pouch. Unlike the storks, the Marabou flies with neck drawn in. The wing beat is slow, but once airborne it is capable of effortless soaring on those broad wings spanning 2.6 m, and is often in company with others of its kind. Inactive for much of the day, spending the time just resting. Can be met with singly or in small parties.

Habitat Not necessarily confined to a watery habitat, frequenting grass covered plains as well as swampy areas, and broad shallow rivers with sandbanks, also the shores of lakes.

Food The Marabou is a stork with vulture-like habits, locating carrion by soaring around. Is well able to drive away vultures when feeding on a carcase in company with others of its kind. Also eats locusts, frogs and small birds.

Voice Has a croaking alarm note. Usually silent except when breeding, when it indulges in bill clapping and produces a variety of grunting sounds.

Display No information except for bill clapping.

Breeding The seasons are variable depending on distribution: January to February in Uganda; June to September in Tanzania; August to January in Kenya; February to April and also August in Nigeria. In most instances breeding coincides with the dry season. A colonial breeder, the nest being constructed in trees or on cliffs. Compared with the bird's size the platform of sticks is not very large. A lining of grass is added before laying the two to three white eggs. Egg size 80 × 51 mm. Incubation period is not recorded. The young have short tufts of hair-like down dotted over head and neck. It is said they are particularly fond of eating 'live' prey in the form of frogs and fish.

Distribution A migratory or partially migratory African species, breeding from Senegal to Sudan, also south to southern parts of the continent, with records from Graaff Reinet, Cradock and Port Elizabeth. Most birds leave breeding area during periods of heavy rain.

Marabou (*Leptoptilus crumeniferus*)

Greater Adjutant Stork
Leptoptilos dubius

Description Standing 120–150 cm to top of head. Upperparts blackish slaty grey with greenish sheen. In breeding plumage only, there is a broad silvery wing band formed by the greater wing coverts and innermost secondaries. Rest of plumage white including a fluffy band of raised feathers around the base of neck. Bill very large and deep at base, gradually tapering towards tip, pale yellow or greeny pink, becoming more reddish at base when breeding. Bare skin of head drab reddish-brown; blackish on front of crown; brick red on back of neck; foreneck yellow, shading to pink on pouch. Much of the bare skin areas are spotted black to some degree. Iris white or yellowish-white. Legs and feet vary from greyish-white to pale fawny brown. Sexes alike.

Characteristics and Behaviour A large and almost repulsive looking stork with a large, naked, pendulous gular pouch 25–35 cm long. The presence of this pouch readily distinguishes it from the Lesser Adjutant Stork (*L. javanicus*). May be encountered singly or in small parties. Spends much time in a hunchbacked attitude or squatting with head drawn well into shoulders and quite often with bill agape. To become airborne a short run is necessary with the enormous wings flapping noisily, but once in flight its progress is quite graceful as it glides and circles high above in company with the vultures. The function of its pendulous pouch is something of a mystery; since it is not connected with the gullet it cannot receive food as would appear to be its purpose.

Habitat Favours marshes and shallow waters, often on the outskirts of villages.

Food Stalks around in marshy areas 'with a martial gait', hence the English name (Adjutant). Although it often feeds on animal carcases along with vultures, its main diet consists of fish, frogs, reptiles, and almost any living creature that it can catch.

Voice The usual bill clapping one associates with this family, also a cow-like 'lowing' and a grunting 'croak'.

Display Has a courtship dance very like that of the Black-necked Stork (*Xenorhynchus asiaticus*).

Breeding The nest is massive platform of sticks some 1–2 m in diameter, and up to 1 m deep, constructed on a horizontal branch high in a tall tree or high in rocky limestone cliffs. Eggs three to four, white and usually heavily tarnished. Size 77 × 58 mm. Both sexes share the incubation (period not recorded), and nest building, probably also the feeding of young. Season varies between October and January depending on the end of rainy season.

Distribution Breeds abundantly in Burma, this being its principal breeding country; also in Thailand, Malaysia, Indochina, Borneo, Sumatra and Java. It is nomadic and a local migrant in the area from Sind in Pakistan through Kutch, northern Gujarat, Rajasthan, Nepal and the Gangetic Plain to Assam and Bangladesh. It is suggested that all Indian Adjutants migrate to the rocky limestone regions along the Ataran River in Pegu district to breed. Not recorded in the southern peninsulas, Sri Lanka and the Andaman Islands.

Lesser Adjutant Stork
(Hair-crested Stork)
Leptoptilos javanicus

Description Standing 110–120 cm to top of head. Plumage of upperparts mainly glossy black, the larger secondary coverts having copper coloured spots towards the tips (when breeding). Head and neck practically naked except for a few hair-like feathers. Bare skin on crown greenish-brown. The naked parts of head and neck yellow but tinged with red during breeding season. Underparts white. Iris white. Bill massive, wedge-shaped and of tarnished yellow. Legs and feet vary from greenish-brown to nearly black. Sexes alike.

Characteristics and Behaviour
Very like a small edition of the Greater Adjutant Stork (*L. dubius*) but upperparts darker and no gular pouch. Has a less erect stance than the Greater Adjutant and is far more wary and difficult to approach. When in flight the sound produced by the wings is not unlike the droning of overhead telegraph wires on a windy day, but one must be close to recognise this. A solitary bird for the most part. Tends not to scavenge quite so readily as the Greater Adjutant.

Habitat   Does not frequent areas close to villages. Favours swampy regions, flooded meadows and forest pools.

Food   Acquires food from shallow waters and marshland. Diet includes fish, frogs, reptiles and crustaceans, also orthopterons such as locusts.

Voice   Apart from a selection of guttural noises similar to those of the White-necked Stork (*Ciconia episcopus*), nothing else is on record.

Display   Similar to the Greater Adjutant Stork.

Breeding   The nest is a very large platform of sticks constructed about 12–30 m high in a forest tree (often *Salmalia*). It measures 120–150 cm across and may attain depths of between 30 and 120 cm depending on the amount of building material added over the years. The three to four white eggs become heavily soiled. Size 76 × 55 mm. Both birds share the incubation (precise period is not on record) and the tending of young. Season extends from November to January.

Distribution   Breeds Burma, Malaysia, Borneo, southern China, Sumatra and Java, Assam, Bengal, Bangladesh, also Delhi, Nepal and Sri Lanka. It is resident, nomadic and makes local migratory movements.

Greater Adjutant Stork

Family—Threskiornithidae

Ibises, Spoonbills
(29 species recorded)

Sacred Ibis
Threskiornis aethiopica

Description   Length 65–75 cm. Head and neck naked dull greyish-black. Plumage predominantly a mixture of pure and dusky white, ornamented with long metallic blue-black scapular plumes that fall loosely in tufts over the closed wing and tail. Both primaries and secondaries tipped with black. Bare skin at sides of breast and underwing deep red. Iris brown, with dark red orbital ring. Bill black, heavy and decurved. Legs and feet black with tinges of red. Sexes alike.

Characteristics and Behaviour   In flight it exhibits a characteristic thin black outline to the broad white wings. The dull dark grey head and neck, and curved bill are also diagnostic. Has a fast wing beat with intermittent glides; neck is held outstretched with legs and feet trailing behind. Perches easily in trees. When walking the gait is slow with body held almost horizontally and neck quite straight, although they often stand with neck retracted. When flying in flocks a V formation or long diagonal lines are adopted.

Habitat   Has adopted a wide range of inland habitats in tropical and subtropical areas, ranging from lakes and rivers to cultivated areas.

Food   Feeds mainly in flocks by wading in shallow watery areas, or occasionally on dry land close to water. Sometimes given to feeding on carrion. Diet consists mainly of invertebrates, including insects, and in particular locusts and grasshoppers. Will also take frogs, reptiles, fish, young birds and eggs.

Voice   Outside the breeding season normally a silent bird, uttering the occasional croak when in flight. It becomes more vocal as breeding commences with both sexes uttering squeaks and moaning sounds, also inhaling and exhaling noises described as 'whoot-whoot, whoot-whooeeoh', 'yuk-pyuk-peuk-pek-peok', or a wheezing 'hnhh-hnhh'. During the final stages of nest building the female often produces a sound resembling 'whaank'. This is uttered sharply and up to three times in succession. When calling to young that have left the nest calls like 'turroh' or 'keerooh' are used.

Display   Courtship activities include bill snapping and stretch displays, with both birds facing each other bowing their heads and extending their necks forwards and downwards finally assuming a normal attitude. Necks and bills may be intertwined and there are occasional bouts of preening.

Breeding   The nest is a large structure of small branches and sticks lined with grasses, rushes, and leaves; the material being collected by the male and fashioned by the female. It may be constructed in a variety of sites from flat-topped thorn trees, low scrub on or just above the ground, amongst rocks, or even in rushy swamps. Two to three rough, dull-white eggs are laid, often having a bluish tinge and usually speckled with red. Size 64 × 42 mm. In Nigeria the breeding season is May to July, and December; in Sudan, July and

Sacred Ibis (*Threskiornis aethiopica*) right.
Glossy Ibis (*Plegadis falcinellus*) left

August; Uganda, February to July, also
November (probably double brooded);
Malawi, September; Kaufe, northern
Zimbabwe, February to August; South
Africa, December. The incubation
period is about 28–29 days, with as little
as 21 days on record! Both birds share
this duty.

Distribution In the western Palearctic it now breeds only in southern
Iraq from Amara to Fao, though definite
nesting records are few. Formerly bred
in Egypt but only prior to 1850. Its present range in Africa is south of the Sahara
from Senegal to the Sudan, Eritrea and
Somalia, south to Cape Province. Other
races of the species are distributed in
Aldabra Island (*T.a. abbotti*) and Madagascar (*T.a. bernieri*).

Oriental Ibis

(White Ibis or Black-headed Ibis)

Threskiornis melanocephala

Description Length 75 cm. Plumage almost entirely white with long ornamental plumes projecting over base of neck. Long plumes of inner secondaries (present only in breeding season) and scapulars pale slaty grey. Head and neck naked, skin bluish-black. Iris red or reddish-brown. Bare skin of flanks and underwings bright red. Bill stout, black, downward curved and not pointed. Legs and feet glossy black. Sexes alike.

Characteristics and Behaviour A large white bird with black head and neck. Gregarious and usually seen in medium to large flocks or small parties, quite often in company with spoonbills or storks. The flight is strong and direct with short intermittent periods of gliding and when airborne the bright red patches of bare skin on flanks and underwings become apparent. A single file or chevron formation is assumed when numbers of birds are flying together, with heads and necks stretched outwards. Tree roosting is the usual practice.

Habitat Frequents flooded farmland, marshes, riverbanks; at times tidal mud-flats and the brackish water of lagoons.

Food Probes for food items, with partly opened bill, in the soft mud of shallow waters, also in boggy areas. The bulk of its diet consists of fish, frogs, molluscs, worms and insects, but there is a small intake of vegetable matter.

Voice Apart from a loud booming sound during the breeding season, and a variety of vibrant grunts, it is by nature a quiet bird.

Display Not on record.

Breeding The nest consists of a stick platform about 25–30 cm across, little or no lining being added. Usually con-structed in a medium-sized tree close to water, sometimes on the very top of a partly submerged bush or shrub, and often quite close to human dwellings. The two to four chalky-white eggs are slightly tinged with pale blue, sometimes with tiny brown spots or blotches but these mostly at the large end. Size 63.5 × 43 mm. Both sexes share the incubation (period thought to be about 23–25 days); they also share nest building and care of the young. Feeding of chicks is by regurgitation, the food being transferred directly from the gullet to the young birds. Breeding season in northern India, June or July to October (depending on time of monsoons); southern India and Sri Lanka, from November to February or March. Both Pallas's Eagle (*Haliaeetus leucoryphus*) and the Spotted Eagle (*Aquila clanga*) regularly prey upon the nestlings.

Distribution Breeds throughout India, Pakistan, Nepal and Sri Lanka. Also Burma and sporadically to China and Japan. Depending on water conditions it is resident, nomadic or locally migratory.

Australian White Ibis

Threskiornis molucca

Description Length 75 cm. A predominantly white bird, with head and half of neck bare and black. On nape are numerous pinkish scorings, and the eye is offset by a pinkish-brown half-moon beneath. Black tips of the main flight feathers glossed with dark green; a few inner wing feathers mottled greenish-black, some elongated and fanned. An area of bare red skin is displayed at the base of the underwing. Iris dark brown. Bill black. Legs purplish-brown, pinkish above knee joint. Sexes alike.

Habitat and Distribution Essentially a bird of freshwater areas, occasionally frequenting brackish and salt water, and favouring swamps, creeks, small pools and dams. Mainly a ground nester but sometimes in trees, breeding in colonies. The nest is built in flooded areas and is constructed of flattened reeds, reinforced with sticks and positioned on a secure area of raised vegetation. A clutch of three or four white eggs is laid. The season is variable and dependent on flood water but in the north it is mainly February to June, in the south September to December. The nominate occurs west Papuan Islands, Kei Islands and New Guinea. *T.m. strictipennis* breeds in the north-western corner of Western Australia, Northern Territory except the southern half, throughout Queensland, New South Wales and Victoria, and the eastern third of South Australia.

Australian White Ibis

Straw-necked Ibis
Threskiornis spinicollis

Description Length 75 cm. Upperparts appear dark; head, throat and upper part of neck black and naked. Eye has a pink semi-circle underneath. Back and wings brownish-black, sheened with bronze, green and purple. Collar around base of neck white. Foreneck and upper breast black but streaked with the yellow shafts of bare feathers. Lower breast, belly and tail white. Bare skin of underwing yellow. Iris dark brown. Bill 15–18 cm long, decurved and black. Legs black but reddish above knee. Sexes alike.

Habitat and Distribution Frequents inland waters and the adjacent grassland regions. Nests in reed beds and other swamp vegetation, occasionally on open ground and in trees. Nest is a platform of trampled-down vegetation and sticks, on which three to four white eggs are laid. The breeding season shows dependence on the flood waters and can be variable, but is usually from April to June in the north, and September to January in the south. Occurs as a breeding species throughout Australia.

Davison's Ibis
(White-shouldered Ibis)
Pseudibis davisoni

Description Length 76 cm. Plumage dark brown with glossy black wings and tail. Similar to Black Ibis (*P. papillosa*) with white patch near shoulder of wing, but no red warty patch on crown.

Habitat and Distribution Frequents marshes, paddy fields, lakes and rivers. Found in south-west China, Borneo, west, central and south Burma, north-west, central and peninsular Thailand, Kampuchea, Cochinchina and Laos.

Giant Ibis

Pseudibis gigantea
(Thaumatibis gigantea)

Description Length 104 cm. A very large, dark greyish-brown bird, tinged with a greenish wash. Head and neck dark brown and naked. Nape and back of neck marked with black bars. Upper wing coverts grey with black scales; primaries black. Bill brown. Legs red. Very similar to Davison's Ibis (*P. davisoni*) but the latter is distinguished by the white patch on the inner lesser wing coverts.

Habitat and Distribution Frequents lakes, swamps and areas of open forest. A rare endemic resident at low elevations throughout its breeding range in central and peninsular Thailand, Kampuchea, Cochinchina and southern and central Laos.

Black Ibis

Black Ibis
(Indian Black Ibis)

Pseudibis papillosa

Description Length 68 cm. Plumage glossy black. Head featherless, black with brilliant red or coral-red warts forming a triangular patch on crown and nape. Small patch of white near shoulder of wing, this being most conspicuous in flight. Iris varies from brownish-yellow to orange-red. Bill slender, downcurved, greyish-green to dull dusky green. Legs and feet brick red. Sexes alike.

Characteristics and Behaviour The white patch near the shoulder of the wing is not always visible in a standing bird. Flight and behaviour very similar to White Ibis (*Eudocimus albus*). Usually seen in small parties of three or four birds, at times in flocks of eight to ten.

Habitat Favours cultivated areas and dry plains; less often frequents marshes and other wet places.

Food Prefers to feed on the dry margins of ponds and lakes, riverbanks, and quite often fields of stubble. Very seldom does it wade to catch its prey. Diet includes small fish (caught from the bank), frogs, earthworms, beetles and a variety of other insects. Also taken, but less frequently, lizards, small snakes, scorpions and crustaceans. Small amounts of grain are sometimes eaten.

Voice A loud nasal call of two or three notes, very similar to the 'kah-hah-hah' of the female Ruddy Shelduck (*Tadornea ferruginea*), usually uttered when in flight. Otherwise a silent species.

Display Not on record.

Breeding Usually a solitary nester but on rare occasions small colonies have been reported, when three to five pairs have used the same tree. The nest is a large platform of sticks 35–60 cm across and 10–15 cm deep, with a loose untidy

lining of straw. Large trees such as ban-
yan or peepul are chosen, or it may be
built in a palmyra palm amongst the
bases of leaf stalks, at heights of between
6 and 12 m. Often the old nests of kites or
vultures may be adopted. Fresh material
is regularly added to the nest during all
stages of incubation. Eggs two to four,
pale bluish-green, most clutches being
thinly spotted and blotched with shades
of pale red, a few have no markings. Size
63 × 49 mm. Both sexes share the incubation, but the period is not on record.
The breeding season varies between
March and October in northern India;
but later in Gujarat, Deccan and the
south.

Distribution   Resident Sind in Pakistan, Gujarat, Rajasthan and throughout
the Gangetic Plain and peninsular India
south to Mysore. Sparingly in Nepal,
Bengal and Assam.

Bald Ibis

Bald Ibis
(Hermit Ibis)

Geronticus eremita

Description   Length 70–80 cm. Head
and throat void of feathers, naked skin
dull crimson. Plumage of neck, entire
body, wings and tail dark metallic
bronzy green, with a purple sheen; only
exception being upper wing coverts
which are shot with shades of violet and
copper. Long pointed hackles on sides
and back of neck give head a shaggy
appearance, forming a wispy ruff. Bill
long, decurved and dull crimson. Legs
shortish; legs and feet dull crimson. Sexes
alike.

Characteristics   and   Behaviour
Even at distance is readily distinguished
from the Glossy Ibis (*Plegadis falcinellus*),
being much larger and of heavier build.
At close quarters the colour of head, bill
and legs are more positive indications.
In flight the less rounded wings become
apparent, as do the three or four short
and well-spaced 'fingers'; the short legs,
even when extended, do not reach tip of
tail. Often glides intermittently with
wings held slightly bowed. A gregarious
species but nowhere plentiful.

Habitat   Unlike other species of ibis,
the Bald Ibis does not frequent lowland
marshes, favouring rivers and coastal regions close to precipitous cliffs, and high
rocky outcrops with ledges and caverns.
However, it can often be seen feeding on
arable fields and other open stretches of
land.

Food   Diet consists chiefly of animal
matter such as locusts, grasshoppers and
crickets, or snakes, lizards, frogs, tadpoles, fish, various rodents, and even
small birds. A daytime feeder, probing
with bill under stones, in crevices and
into tussocky vegetation. Will also take
berries, various weeds and shoots, and
rhizomes of aquatic plants.

Voice   When feeding mostly silent, but

101

at the nest and when visiting roosts, can be very vocal. Among the calls are a guttural 'jum' or 'jupe', a somewhat raucous 'harr-harr' and a disyllabic 'couahh, yooohhh'.

Display During threat display the feathers of mantle and neck are raised, with head retracted, bill agape and lifted. This is followed by quickly extending neck and lowering bill to ground. During courtship display, bill is pointed upward and neck extended, throat becomes enlarged as disyllabic call is produced, lowering bill to touch breast on first note, raising it rapidly for second note. Also sways body from one foot to the other with hackles raised.

Breeding Season principally April to May or early June. Nests colonially on rocky cliffs along river courses in semi-desert regions, often in company with other species such as Lesser Kestrels, Choughs, and Black Kites. A loosely constructed platform of twigs is built on a rocky ledge, and three bluish-white eggs are laid at intervals of from 1 to 3 days. Size 63 × 44 mm. Both sexes share the incubation for a period of 24–25 days.

Distribution Range is not fully known. Breeds locally in Morocco, northern Algeria, northern Iraq, southern Egypt, the Sudan and Ethiopia, possibly also in the Yemen. Those breeding in Turkey winter in north-east Africa; Ethiopian breeders winter chiefly in the Massawa/Asmara region. The wintering grounds of the Moroccan birds are not known, but it is thought they may travel south, crossing the Sahara, presumably staying inland rather than visiting coastal regions. *G. calvus* of South Africa is synonymous with *G. eremita*.

Japanese Crested Ibis
Nipponia nippon

Description Length 76 cm. In breeding plumage mainly a white bird with a bushy crest; but flight feathers, underside of wings and tail pale pink. Naked skin on face red. Bill long and downcurved, black with red tip. Legs and feet dark red. Sexes alike.

Characteristics and Behaviour In flight is readily distinguished from all the 'white' egrets by its extended neck, downcurved bill, red facial skin and legs that do not project beyond tail. Has quicker wing beats than the egrets. When numbers are flying together they assume a V or line formation.

Habitat Frequents swampy regions in dense forest.

Food Forages in swamps and ponds, also paddy fields at elevation. Takes small fishes, pond snails, frogs and aquatic insects. Freshwater crabs are also on record.

Voice A call not unlike that of the Raven, a nasal 'guah'.

Display Not recorded.

Breeding Extends from April to May. A platform of sticks is constructed on branches high in a tree. The normal clutch is 2 to 3 eggs, greenish blue in colour and spotted with brown. Size not recorded, but incubation period is said to be about 30 days.

Distribution Resident in Japan where it was once widely distributed. The widespread hunting of this ibis in the 19th century reduced the population to such an extent that between 1890 and 1930 it was thought to be extinct. However, in the 1930s small numbers were found breeding in central Honshu on the Noto Peninsula, and a few others on Sado Island in Niigata Prefecture. These populations are now protected by law as a Special Natural Monument. However, during the 1940s clearance of vast areas of forest destroyed much of the species' natural habitat and by 1960 only twelve birds were thought to be left, two of which were found dead following the severe winter of 1960/61. In former years the Japanese Crested Ibis has bred in eastern Siberia, Manchuria and northern China, though by no means commonly. These populations were not resident (as are the Japanese birds) but wintered in southern China and Hainan. It is possible that a colony may still exist in China today, and the need for protection is all the more important.

Wattled Ibis
Bostrychia carunculata

Description Length 65–75 cm. In size, general appearance and overall colour, very like the Olive Ibis (*B. olivacea*) but can be immediately identified by the diagnostic white wing coverts. The face is feathered and a wattle hangs from throat. Sexes alike.

Habitat and Distribution Frequents swamps and areas of high moorland. The nest is built in trees or bushes protruding from cliff faces, and is a structure of sticks lined with strips of bark and grass stems, in which two dirty white eggs are laid. Breeding season in Ethiopia is from April to July. Breeding range is in eastern Africa, lying in the highlands of Ethiopia from Senafe to Shoa, Maji, Alghe and Burgi; also recorded from the coast of Eritrea.

Wattled Ibis

Hadada Ibis

Bostrychia hagedash
(Hagedashia hagedash)

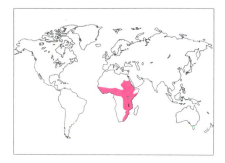

Description Length 76 cm. Overall appearance drab dark greyish-brown, although there is a prominent green iridescence on the wing coverts. Eye offset by a whitish stripe underneath. Flight feathers and tail display an iridescent bluish-black. Bill long, black and decurved, with red at the base extending about half way along the upper mandible. Legs blackish-brown; feet pale orange brown. Sexes alike although female slightly smaller with a shorter bill. *B.h. brevirostris* differs from the nominate in having darker underparts, greener wing coverts and a longer bill. *B.h. nilotica* resembles *B.h. brevirostris* but has a characteristically longer bill.

Characteristics and Behaviour From a distance it superficially resembles the Glossy Ibis (*Plegadis falcinellus*). However the Hadada is much larger and of heavier build. Unlike other closely related African species it lacks any form of crest. In flight the bill projects downwards, with the legs and feet not projecting beyond the tail. The heavy beats of its broad rounded wings are sometimes interspersed with short glides. More solitary than most ibis species and tending to be quite tame. When disturbed it often alights in a neighbouring tree.

Habitat The least aquatic of all African ibises, frequenting streams, marshes and pasturelands, also favouring timbered areas and occasionally being found in the glades of deep forests. Cultivated land seems to be an attraction and they are quite commonly seen around small towns and villages.

Hadada Ibis (*Bostrychia hagedash*)

Food It is not dependent on watery areas for food and often feeds well away from wet places, seeming content to probe lawns and grasslands with its long curved bill as it searches for insects, worms and snails.

Voice The bird's name is derived from its raucous call of 'ha-ha-a-a-a-a', usually uttered on the wing. At dawn its rattling croaks are a well-known feature.

Display No information.

Breeding The nest is a platform of twigs and small branches lined with dry grass and usually built in trees at heights below 9 m and close to water; sometimes trees on cliff faces and the old nests of other birds are used. Three eggs are laid, greenish-grey, spotted and blotched with chestnut. Size 51 × 45 mm. In equable tropical climates such as Lake Victoria breeding occurs throughout the year, peak laying coinciding with the early and main periods of rain. In South Africa eggs are laid mainly from September to November. Incubation continues for about 26 days by both sexes.

Distribution In many parts of tropical and southern Africa it is the commonest ibis. It ranges from Senegal to eastern Zaire, and from the Sudan to the eastern Cape; not being found around the lower Congo River nor in the dry south-western areas. Although it does not occur along the southern edge of the western Sahara in the Steppe areas, it does occur further north around the Nile. *B.h. brevirostris* breeds in Central and West Africa. *B.h. nilotica* is a South African subspecies. *B.h. erlangeri* occurs from Somalia to Malawi.

Olive Ibis
(Green Ibis)

Bostrychia olivacea
(Lampribis olivacea)

Description Length 65–75 cm. Upperparts drab iridescent green, occasionally showing a pinkish cast. Wing coverts much brighter iridescent greeny bronze and rose. Nape displays a crest similar to that of the Hammerhead Stork (*Scopus umbretta*). Underparts brownish with only a slight amount of greenish tinge. Similar in appearance to the Hadada Ibis (*B. hagedash*) but in general is a much darker bird. Sexes alike.

Habitat and Distribution Frequents thick mountain forest at fairly high altitudes, and it can generally be said that any ibis seen at over 2100 m within its range, will be of this species. The nest is a construction of dead sticks placed at a considerable height in a tree; probably also nests in holes in cliff faces. At least three eggs are laid. The season for Kenya seemingly between June and August. The nominate breeds from Sierra Leone to Liberia. *B.o. cupreipennis* breeds southern Cameroon to western Zaire. *B.o. rothschildi* breeds on Príncipe. *B.o. bocagei* breeds on Sao Thomé. *B.o. akleyorum* breeds Kenya, northern Tanzania and eastern Zaire.

Spot-breasted Ibis
Bostrychia rara

Description Length 47 cm. Upperparts in general dark green. Crown dusky green, displaying a long cinnamon-buff crest. Lower back, rump and uppertail coverts black, tinged with bluish-green. Tail purplish-black with greenish tinge. Lesser and median wing coverts reddish-purple with a slight greenish gloss; greater coverts black, glossed with purple. Back and the inner secondaries green. Sides of face, cheeks and upper part of throat dusky brown. Back of neck, sides of neck and underparts of body cinnamon brown, all the feathers broadly margined with either dull green or greenish-brown. Under tail coverts, under wing coverts and axillaries black with a greenish iridescence, the axillaries with a purple sheen. Naked skin around eye and lores black. Iris dark brown. Bill blackish. Legs and feet dirty yellow.

Habitat and Distribution Frequents the forest districts of West Africa from Liberia to Gabon and Príncipe.

Plumbeous Ibis
Harpiprion caerulescens

Description Length 75 cm. General colour above whitish-grey, with subterminal markings of dusky brown tinged with green, producing a mottled effect. Wing coverts like the back; greater coverts dusky, edged with hoary grey; bastard wing and primary coverts black glossed with green or purple; inner secondaries like the back. Dusky tail feathers glossed with a darker green, upper tail coverts glossy olive green. Head and face have dull ash-coloured feathers, and there is a frontal white band that narrows centrally on the forehead. Long narrow crest feathers whitish-grey with ash-coloured centres; feathers on sides of neck and lower throat similarly coloured. Throat dusky grey; rest of underparts whitish-grey; under tail coverts darker with fine dusky lines; under wing coverts and axillaries a somewhat darker grey. Lores and naked chin black. Iris orange. Bill and legs blackish; toes reddish-yellow.

Distribution Breeds from central Brazil to Paraguay and Argentina.

Buff-necked Ibis
(White-throated Ibis)
Theristicus caudatus

Description Length 74 cm. Head, neck and upper breast buffy white, tinged with cinnamon. Rest of upperparts pale purplish-grey. Secondaries and greater wing coverts white; primaries black. Throat white and margined on either side by a dark brown line. Lower breast and belly blackish-grey. Iris orange red. Bill long, black and decurved. Legs and feet orange. There are four races (including the nominate): *T.c. hyperorius* is similar to the nominate in size and proportions but is somewhat paler, more brownish beneath and the tail tends to have a steel-green tinge. Branicki's Ibis (*T.c. branickii*) has paler breast and central abdomen than *T.c. hyperorius* or the nominate; chest band grey; greater wing coverts grey (not white); foreneck and breast more creamy white than buff. Usually more extensive feathering on throat; wings, tail and bill shorter. Blacked-faced Ibis (*T.c. melanopsis*) differs from *T.c. branickii* (the other mountain race) in its white wing coverts and rich buff foreneck and breast. Throat feathering is more restricted, occasionally limited to chin only.

Habitat and Distribution Frequents open swampy regions and savanna areas along the borders of lakes and rivers, also favours thin forest coverings up to about 500 m above sea level. They are colonial breeders, the nest being a bulky construction of sticks usually placed in a tree. Breeds in the tropical zone of Guiana, French Guiana, northern Venezuela from Zulia to Monagas, Colombia south to Valle and Meta, and practically throughout Brazil although the southern limit is uncertain. *T.c. hyperorius* breeds in Bolivia at Cochabamba and Santa Cruz, southern Brazil, Paraguay, Uruguay and northern Argentina. *T.c. branickii* breeds in the puna zone of Ecuador and Peru, north-western Bolivia, and the mountains of Arica in northern Chile. *T.c. melanopsis* breeds in coastal Peru (Lima) south through Chile and southern Argentina to Tierra del Fuego. During the winter Patagonian birds migrate northwards to northern Argentina, Chile and Peru.

Green Ibis
(Cayenne Ibis)

Mesembrinibis cayennensis

Description Length 58 cm. Crown dark greyish-green with a bushy nuchal crest. Neck metallic bottle green, somewhat darker on throat. Facial area grey. Rest of upperparts a variegated shade of dark and pale green tinged with rustic yellow-brown. Underparts dusky purple. Iris red. Bill blackish and slightly decurved. Legs and feet dark green.

Habitat and Distribution Favours wet and muddy areas of wooded terrain. A colonial nester building a frail-looking structure of twigs high in a tree. Its breeding range includes northern Colombia from the lower Atrato River eastwards to Arauca and Meta; the basins of the Orinoco and Apure Rivers in Venezuela; the Guianas southwards, east of the Andes to Peru; Brazil to Amazonas, Mato Grosso and São Paulo; Paraguay and Argentina.

Bare-faced Ibis
(Whispering Ibis)

Phimosus infuscatus

Description Length 48 cm. Overall plumage greenish-black, the wings displaying a bluish-green tinge. Feathers of hindneck have a strong purplish gloss. Facial skin reddish. Iris pale brown. Bill clay coloured. Legs pinkish-white. There are three races (including the nominate): *P.i. berlepschi* has steel-green feathers on hindneck, deep carmine facial skin and a reddish-brown bill with a blackish tip. *P.i. nudifrons* has a clay-coloured bill and brick-red facial skin.

Habitat and Distribution Frequents open fields and pastures, wooded swamps and streams near sea level. A colonial breeder, the nest being a crude flat platform of sticks and twigs built in a low tree and appearing very small for the size of the bird, only 30–35 cm across. The nominate breeds from Beni to Santa Cruz in north-eastern Bolivia, Paraguay, Uruguay, and in Argentina south to Tucumán, Córdoba and Buenos Aires. *P.i. berlepschi* breeds east of the Rio Sinú in northern Colombia, eastern Ecuador, Venezuela south to north-western Amazonas and Bolivar, Guyana, Surinam, and Rio Branco in north-western Brazil. *P.i. nudifrons* breeds central and eastern Brazil from central and northern Mato Grosso, Maranhão, Piauí, and Bahía southward.

White Ibis

Eudocimus albus

Description Length 56–58.5 cm. In breeding plumage a predominantly white bird with black wing tips and a scarlet face. Bill, legs and feet also scarlet. During autumn and into the early part of winter crown and hindneck become duskily mottled, and the face, bill, legs and feet become a dull pinkish colour.

During nuptial display the gular pouch is noticeably distended. Sexes alike.

Habitat and Distribution Frequents those vast marshy regions with lakes, ponds and floating boggy islets, overgrown with water hyacinths and other vegetation. Occurs also in the swampy forested borders of river valleys. Nests colonially in mangroves at heights of 2.5–4.5 m, from March to August. The four eggs are bluish or greenish-white. Apart from a slight movement in the USA during spring, the White Ibis is a resident species throughout its range, occurring in coastal regions of Mexico, Central America, north-west South America and the Greater Antilles (with the exception of Puerto Rico), Curaçao and Trinidad. Also from Texas to South Carolina.

White Ibis

Scarlet Ibis
Eudocimus ruber

Description Length 56 cm. In the adult birds, apart from the dark blue tips of four outer primaries, plumage deep scarlet, the larger feathers having white shafts. Bare facial skin a little duller in shade than the plumage. Bill dark, 16.5 cm long and decurved. Legs and feet pink. Sexes alike but female slightly smaller.

Habitat and Distribution Occurs in coastal mangroves, swamps and marshy areas; also mudflats and estuaries. During very dry periods flocks may vacate the coastal areas in preference for inland areas higher up the rivers. A colonial nester with a preference for river mouth mangroves. The nest is a loose platform of sticks constructed at heights of about 2 m above ground level. Two to four eggs are laid. The season extends from about June to October. The full extent of its range is not known because access to many of the probable breeding areas is extremely difficult. Inhabits coastal regions of northern and eastern South America extending from Venezuela to eastern Brazil and Trinidad. Breeding colonies are known only in Trinidad, Venezuela and Surinam, but outside this range the Scarlet Ibis is occasionally reported from Cuba, Grenada and Jamaica.

Sharp-tailed Ibis
Cercibis oxycerca

Description Length 76 cm. Plumage glossy greenish-black with sheens of purple on the back; displays a bushy occipital crest. Bare ocular region orangey red, as are bill and legs.

Habitat and Distribution Favours areas of savanna along the borders of lakes and rivers; also open marshy regions. Breeds in Guyana; in the llanos along the Orinoco and Apure Rivers in Venezuela; east of the Andes in Colombia in the llanos along the Casanarem Cravo Norte and Arauca Rivers; western Amazonian Brazil north of the Amazon along the Rio Negro and Rio Branco, and southwards to north-western Mato Grosso along the Guaporé River.

Glossy Ibis

Plegadis falcinellus

(Illustrated with Sacred Ibis, *Threskiornis aethiopica*, on left)

Description Length 63.5 cm. In breeding plumage upperparts deep chestnut or maroon brown but glossed with greens and purples. Tail black and similarly glossed. Underparts rich chestnut with deep purple under tail coverts and axillaries. Non-breeding adults have brown head and neck streaked with white, scapulars and innermost wing coverts glossy greenish-blue. Iris either grey, brown, or a mottled combination of these colours. Bill slender, downward curved, dark olive-grey or grey-brown, with a patch of bare lead-blue skin at base. Naked skin of face and around eyes lead coloured. Legs and feet bronzy brown, but bluish above the knee. Sexes alike. The White-faced subspecies *P.f. chihi* (often regarded as a separate species, *P. chihi*) has a white edging to the bare facial skin.

Characteristics and Behaviour The smaller size and dark brown legs distinguish the Glossy Ibis from both the Black Ibis (*Pseudibis papillosa*) and the Giant Ibis (*Pseudibis gigantea*) and it does not have the white patch on the wing shoulder as does the Black. At a distance resembles a very dark Curlew. Usually quite tame, even confiding; gregarious at all times, occurring in flocks of up to 40 or 50 birds. The flight is on rapidly beating wings with intermittent glides, and when in flocks a chevron (or sometimes an echelon-like) formation is assumed. Regularly uses trees for roosting. Other habits as for White Ibis (*Eudocimus albus*) and Black Ibis. Walks in the same sedate manner as the spoonbill. Can swim short distances if necessity demands.

Habitat Frequents large ponds, lakes, riverbanks, marshy areas, floodlands and deltas. Occasionally shallow coastal beaches.

Food Usually feeds in small flocks. Included in the diet are molluscs, crustaceans, worms, small frogs and probably tadpoles, but insects and their larvae form the greater part. Food is acquired in a similar manner to that of the White Ibis; searching in marshes, or wading belly-deep in the shallows often completely immersing the head as it probes the mud for food.

Voice During the breeding season, a deep crow-like croak 'graa graa graa' and a bleat very like that of a sheep or calf. Otherwise a seemingly silent bird.

Display At the nest mutual bowing takes place and the occasional preening of one bird by its mate; little else is on record.

Breeding The season extends from May to July. The nest is a small collection of sticks, 30 cm across and about 12 cm deep, often in a tree or bush, or in deep reed beds and constructed of reed stems. In both cases a lining of green vegetation is often added. Always built above or close to water. Eggs two to three in India and Pakistan, more often three to four (five) in Europe and North America. They are deep blue-green to pale blue. Size 52 × 37 mm. Both sexes share the incubation for a period of 21 days. Fledging period 30 days with the young staying in vicinity of nest for a further 20 days or so. Both adults share the nest building and care of young.

Distribution Widespread. Breeds in southern Europe, the Mediterranean and Middle Eastern countries, Baluchistan, Afghanistan, Turkestan. In isolated areas from Sind (Pakistan) across northern India to Assam, including Nepal, Orissa, Manipur and Bangladesh, Burma, south-eastern China, Borneo and Java. Also East Africa, Madagascar, south-western North America, the Greater Antilles and south to central South America. In winter the Glossy Ibis moves south from North America to tropical regions of South America from

Brazil and Peru, south to Argentina and Chile. From the Mediterranean and southern Europe many move south into Africa where they frequent the marshlands and great lakes of the interior. Others remain throughout the winter on both the northern and southern Mediterranean coasts. *P.f. peregrinus* inhabits the Philippines, Indonesia and Australia. *P.f. chihi* is found in southern Texas, southern Louisiana and occasionally in Florida. Also on to southern Mexico.

Puna Ibis
(Andean Glossy Ibis)
Plegadis ridgwayi

Description Length 60 cm. In breeding plumage head, neck and mantle chestnut brown. Rest of upperparts iridescent green, bronze and violet. Underparts fulvous with a faint purple gloss. In non-breeding attire head and neck finely striped with black and white; underparts slightly mixed with grey. Bill blackish and slightly downcurved. Legs and feet brownish-grey.

Habitat and Distribution A bird of high mountainous regions, frequenting the shores of lagoons and other marshy regions in the puna zone. It is very rarely seen on the coast. Breeds in the puna zone of the Andes in Peru from Junin southwards to Bolivia in La Paz, Cochabamba and Oruro; recorded from Jujuy in north-western Argentina (once); also the Cordillera de Arica in northern Chile.

Crested Wood Ibis
(White-winged Ibis)
Lophotibis cristata

Description Length 70 cm. Upperparts cinnamon brown. Wings entirely white except for black of innermost secondaries. Back, lower back, rump, upper tail coverts and tail all black but with a

slight purplish gloss. Central feathers of crest sandy buff, rest purplish-brown or glossy steel-coloured as are feathers on side of neck. Sides of face naked. Cheeks and throat blackish, the throat adorned with a few steel-green feathers. From the foreneck downwards the rest of underparts dull cinnamon, somewhat lighter on the abdomen. Primary coverts and those on bend of wing white. Under wing coverts, axillaries, and under tail coverts black, slightly glossed with purple. Bare skin around eye red. Iris reddish. Bill green. Legs and feet dark red.

Habitat and Distribution Usually seen in pairs walking about the forest floor; quite inconspicuous. When flushed will often perch in a nearby tree; during flight the white wings are very striking. Not restricted to damp places or the vicinity of streams. Feeds on insects, spiders and worms. November is thought to be included in its breeding season, exact period not recorded. Occurs from sea level to 1800 m in the forests of the Oriental and Northern Savanna of Madagascar. Common in the dense forests of the Oriental Province, especially near the sea 20 km south-west of Maroantsetra. The Western White-winged Ibis (*L.c. urschi*) is found only in the Western Savanna, but in the northern part of its range it is intergraded with *L.c. cristata*. At Tabiky it is common and often seen in the more densely wooded areas of the wooded plain and along the small streams, bordered by gallery forest in the limestone areas.

Roseate Spoonbill
Platalea ajaja
(*Ajaia ajaja*)

Description Length 76–86 cm. Adult plumage predominantly pinkish, but has a white neck and streaks of red from bend of wing to the back. Head almost completely featherless, naked

110

skin greenish. Bill long, spatulate, brownish. Legs and feet red. Sexes alike.

Habitat and Distribution Inhabits mangrove swamps, saline lagoons and coastal waters. The Roseate Spoonbill is at least 3 years old before breeding. A colonial nester with male collecting most of the material and female building the platform nest in a tree or bush. Eggs laid November in Florida, and April in Texas. Breeds from southern coast of USA, through Central America, the West Indies (on larger islands), and in many parts of South America down to Argentina (but nowhere plentiful).

African Spoonbill

Platalea alba
(Illustrated with Yellow-billed Stork, *Ibis ibis*, on right)

Description Similar to the White Spoonbill (*P. leucorodia*) but differs in having no yellowish patch on foreneck. Bare facial skin red; legs bright pink; usually a little red on the upper mandible.

Distribution Breeds from Gambia to Sudan, and Cape Province.

Yellow-billed Spoonbill
Platalea flavipes

Description Length 100 cm. Plumage almost completely white but some of flight feathers are tipped with black. When breeding has long hackles on lower part of foreneck. Facial skin lilac blue, narrowly edged with black. Iris pale yellow or whitish. Bill yellow, long and spatulate. Legs and feet yellow. Sexes alike.

Habitat and Distribution Frequents swamps and marshes, both coastal and inland. Constructs platform nest of sticks and vegetation, at varying heights in bushes or trees standing in or close to water, or on the ground amongst dense aquatic vegetation. Gregarious, often in mixed colonies. The season varies with the rains, nests are recorded for most months. Breeds New South Wales, Queensland, all but the southwest of Northern Territory, eastern South Australia, also western and northern regions of Western Australia.

Yellow-billed Spoonbill

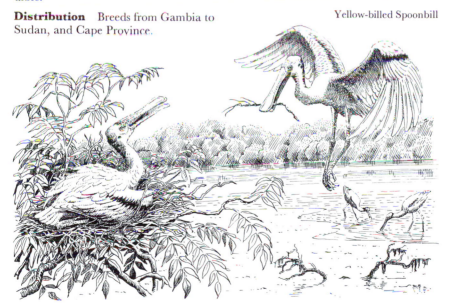

White Spoonbill

Platalea leucorodia

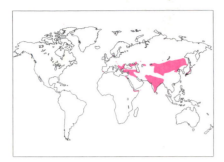

Description   Length 86 cm. Standing 61 cm to top of head. Plumage entirely white but for yellow patch on lower part of foreneck. When breeding has a nuchal crest of long and bushy white feathers which can be raised during periods of emotional stress, as when angry or during breeding display. Neck long. Bill very distinctive, long, flat and spatula-shaped, upper mandible black, terminating in a bright yellow spoon-shape, lower mandible slaty grey and of a similar shape. Bare skin of face and throat canary or sulphur yellow, occasionally with black blotches in loral region. Legs and feet black, the long toes webbed at base. Iris varies from dark brown to deep brownish-red. Sexes alike but females have smaller bills and shorter legs.

Characteristics and Behaviour

More closely related to the ibises than the herons. When in flight the neck is not drawn in but is fully extended, the long spatulate bill giving the bird the appearance of being 'off balance'. The flight would seem to be rather slow and laboured, a loose echelon formation or broken V being adopted when several birds are travelling together. At all times a gregarious and quite a sociable species, met with either in small parties or in flocks of up to 50 or 60 birds, often in the company of egrets, ibises, herons or other species of similar habit. Often utilises heat thermals, soaring very high.

Habitat   Frequents marshland, rivers and especially large lagoons with dense marginal vegetation, such as reeds and bushes. Occasionally visits mangrove swamps and tidal creeks.

Food   Crepuscular in habit, feeding during the early morning hours and in the evenings rather than broad daylight. Acquires food by wading into shallow water at the edge of a lagoon or swamp, and sweeping bill with partly open mandibles from side to side in the water. Diet includes small fish, tadpoles, aquatic insects, frogs and molluscs. When food is abundant in one spot, they will often be seen feeding in tightly grouped parties, all avidly contesting for the prey, searching methodically backwards and forwards. Has a loping run.

Voice   When breeding bill clattering occurs and low grunting noises are occasionally heard. Otherwise very silent.

Display   Little has been recorded apart from raising the crest and pointing the bill upwards. Also mutual preening.

Breeding   Nests in colonies, even mixed ones, but within these the spoonbills tend to segregate themselves from other species, and defend the immediate territory around the nest. Season variable in the Indian subcontinent depending on time of monsoon, usually July to October in northern India; November to January in southern India; December to April in Sri Lanka; mid-March to mid-April in Europe. The nest is a platform of sticks and reed stems, lined with grasses and leaves, and built in reed beds or in trees partly submerged in marshy areas. The three or four eggs are chalky white, long oval in shape pointed at one end, and sparsely blotched and spotted with varying shades of brown. Size 66 × 44 mm. Both birds sharing the incubation for about 21 days.

Distribution   In Europe the breeding strongholds must be in the marismas at

White Spoonbill (*Platalea leucorodia*)

the mouth of the Guadalupejo in the area between Gibraltar and Jerez, southern Spain. Also breeds in the Netherlands along the dune coastline on Texel and at lakes such as at the Naarder Meer Reserve; Denmark at the Linfjarden; Austria; Hungary (Neuricoll); Kisbalaton; Valence; also over a wide range chiefly around the Danube in south-eastern Europe; Central Asia from China, southern Transbaikalia, Ussuriland and Japan; south to Syria, Egypt, India and Taiwan; coastal regions of Eritrea and northern Somalia. Partly resident and nomadic, partly winter visitor in Pakistan and Bangladesh and practically all of India, Nepal, and Sri Lanka. Eastern European birds probably migrate to the southern Mediterranean and tropical West Africa.

Royal Spoonbill
Platalea regia

Description Length 75 cm. When breeding plumage white with long ornamental nuchal plumes, 15 cm long. Foreneck slightly sandy buff. At other times crest absent and plumage sandy buff. Facial skin black, also has small patches of naked reddish-orange skin above and below eyes, and on forehead. Iris dark red. Bill long, black and spatulate. Legs and feet black. Sexes alike.

Habitat and Distribution Inhabits both coastal and inland swamps, and marshes. Breeding season chiefly October to April, when a platform of sticks and vegetation is built in a tree or bush, growing in or close to a swamp; also nests on ground in dense vegetation of swamp. Breeds north-east corner of Western Australia; and all but the south-west corner of Northern Territory, throughout Queensland, New South Wales, Victoria and eastern third of South Australia. The species extends to New Zealand, New Guinea and the Celebes.

Royal Spoonbill

Black-faced Spoonbill
Platalea minor

Description Very similar to the White Spoonbill (*P. leucorodia*) but 7.5 cm smaller. Also differs in its entirely grey bill and black facial skin.

Distribution Breeds East Asia, eastern China, Hainan, Taiwan and the Philippines.

Family—Phoenicopteridae

Flamingos
(5 species recorded)

Lesser Flamingo
Phoeniconaias minor

Description Standing 90–105 cm to top of head. Distinguished from *Phoenicopterus ruber roseus* by its smaller size, crimson feathers at base of dark coloured bill, and plumage of a deeper rosy pink. Similar in having black flight feathers on otherwise crimson wings. The crimson on back and breast of male bird is lacking in the female. Bill massive, downward curved, dusky red with a black tip. Iris red. Legs and feet a brighter red than in the Greater. Female a little paler and somewhat smaller than the male.

Characteristics and Behaviour A gregarious species often seen in very large numbers along with *P.r. roseus*. In flight the crimson and black of underwings is very striking, neck comparatively thick, and trailing legs shorter than in *P.r. roseus.*

Habitat Seems more restricted to tidal lagoons, also salt and brackish waters, than is *P.r. roseus.*

Food Shows more of a preference for feeding in concentrated brine than its larger relative, wading to depths of 30–45 cm. Feeds almost entirely on algae and diatoms which it filters from the water using its highly modified bill structure. With its head and inverted bill partially or wholly immersed, the bird uses a side to side scything motion, sucking in water which is then forced out through lamellae on which the microscopic organisms are caught. Insect larvae and copepods are also occasionally taken. Flamingos regularly drink fresh water.

Voice When feeding along with others of its own kind, a continuous babbling sound can be detected. It probably also has the honk-like call of the Greater Flamingo.

Display Prior to breeding dance-like displays by flocks of birds may be seen, both on the breeding grounds and at feeding areas. Nothing else seems to have been recorded.

Breeding Probably commences during April and on to June or July. Nests colonially in open areas of mudflats, often along with *P.r. roseus*. A mound of mud is constructed to a height of 20–30 cm, being broad at the base and tapering slightly upwards, with a central depression on the top; nests are usually close together. The clutch consists of one to three chalky-white eggs, with an incubation period of 28 days. Young birds are fed by both adults on regurgitated algae, until such time as their own filtration system develops; they remain in or close to the nest for several weeks. Breeding is intermittent, with a population of Lesser Flamingos nesting on average about once in three years.

Distribution The Rift Valley lakes in East Africa and the pans (particularly Etosha) north of the Kalahari in southern Africa are the main breeding grounds. The species was first discovered on Lake Natron in 1954 and on several occasions since then up to 500,000 pairs have nested there. Also breeds in Madagascar, and the Rann of Kutch in northwestern India.

Chilean Flamingo

Phoenicopterus chilensis

Description Length 100–110 cm. Distinguished from the Andean Flamingo (*Phoenicoparrus andinus*) (of which it is sometimes regarded as a subspecies) by its more roseate colour, much less conspicuous black primaries, and lack of any vinaceous areas on its neck. (It is also considered by some to be a race of *Phoenicopterus ruber*). Iris pale yellow. Bill, terminal half black, basal half whitish. Legs greenish-grey to light blue, dark red at joints and toes. Immature birds have yellowish legs with bluish-red joints.

Habitat and Distribution Breeds in the central and southern highlands of Peru; also similar regions of Chile from Tarpaca to Magalanes; in Bolivia; Paraguay; Brazil (Rio Grande do Sul); and throughout Argentina where it breeds mainly in the mountains and in the south. Birds winter in Tierra del Fuego.

116

Andean Flamingo
Phoenicoparrus andinus

Description Length from bill to tail 110–120 cm. Roseate in colour with vinaceous areas on neck. Conspicuous black on primaries which is more noticeable on folded wing than in James' Flamingo (*P. jamesi*) or Chilean Flamingo (*Phoenicopterus chilensis*). Bare facial skin violet red. Iris dark. Bill relatively short and deep, pale yellowish-white with terminal half black. Legs yellow, knee joints red; only three toes on each foot. Flies with neck extended and legs stretched out behind.

Habitat and Distribution A bird mainly of the high altitudes, not less than 2300 m, where it frequents marshes and salt lakes. A colonial nester sometimes with up to 2000 birds. The nest is a conical mound typical of the flamingos, and a single white egg is laid. In Chile it breeds in the high altitude zone from the Peruvian border to Salar de Maricunga, the Atacama, also similar regions in north-western Argentina, western Bolivia, and the extreme south of Peru. Migrates to lower altitudes in winter.

James' Flamingo
(Puna Flamingo or Lesser Andean Flamingo)
Phoenicoparrus jamesi

Description Length from bill to tail 90 cm. Resembles the Andean Flamingo (*P. andinus*) but smaller and paler, with tertials pinkish-red not black. On folded wing, black of flight feathers much less conspicuous. Generally much less roseate than the Chilean Flamingo (*Phoenicopterus chilensis*), but at close quarters can be distinguished immediately by its brick-red legs, also by the smaller and relatively shorter bill which is yellowish-orange with the terminal third black, and is slightly curved to the left. Bare loral area bright red. Iris orange.

Habitat and Distribution Inhabits salt lakes and marshes of high altitudes where it breeds in mixed colonies with both the Andean and Chilean Flamingos. Occurs in Chile, breeding in the Andean regions of Antofagasta and Tarapaca, in north-western Argentina, and across the Bolivian plateau to the puna zone of south-western Peru.

Andean Flamingo and the smaller
James' Flamingo

Greater Flamingo
Phoenicopterus ruber

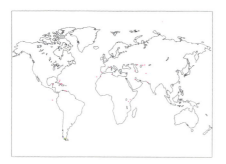

Description Standing 140 cm to top of head. A long-necked bird with flame pink and crimson plumage. Wings black and bright scarlet. Bill massive, pink with black tip, becoming downcurved about midway along its length. Facial and gular skin pale pink. Iris lemon yellow. Legs long and pink, the shade variable as in the bill. Female paler and a little smaller than the male. The nominate is by far the most richly coloured subspecies. *P.r. roseus* has a chiefly rosy-white plumage with the black and scarlet wings. *P. chilensis*, which is sometimes treated as a subspecies of *P. ruber*, has plumage of a deeper pink than *P.r. roseus* but is paler than the nominate.

Characteristics and Behaviour In flight the black and red underwings coupled with its large size, long outstretched legs and slender neck, are diagnostic. Very gregarious, met with in flocks of varying size. When flying may occur in single file, a loosely formed echelon, or in V formation. At rest usually stands on one leg with neck coiled and head tucked into back feathers.

Habitat Frequents salt pans, marshes, brackish lakes and lagoons, also coastal mudflats.

Food Usually feeds in shallow brackish waters, but sometimes in concentrated brine. In favourite feeding areas, vast numbers of birds are seen to congregate. Food is acquired by immersing the head and inverted bill, and employing a skimming or scraping action. Water is sucked in by a piston-like movement of the fleshy tongue, food particles being filtered out through the lamellae along the edges of the bill. Often the head and bill describe a feeding circle in the mud of about 60–90 cm in diameter. The diet includes larvae, crustaceans, small molluscs, plant seeds and quite possibly the occasional small fish.

Voice A goose-like 'honk', usually uttered when in flight. Also a continuous babbling sound when feeding in numbers.

Display Not recorded.

Breeding The season varies considerably throughout its distribution depending on water conditions. September and October to March and April, often at intervals of 9 months, close to the Equator; in more temperate zones every 12 months. However in the Camargue nesting occurs at intervals of 2 years, on average. The nest is a mound of mud scraped up to a height of 50 cm, tapering towards the top with a shallow depression to receive the single whitish to pale blue egg (sometimes two). Size 89 × 54.5 mm. Both sexes share the incubation for a period of 30–32 days. Nests are built in hundreds and closely positioned one to another, over areas of several acres. The newly hatched chicks are fed on a clear liquid solution from the adults bill. Rising water levels, undue noise, or excessive disturbance by animals or humans can cause an entire breeding population to forsake their nests.

Distribution The nominate is restricted in breeding range to northern Yucatán in Mexico. Also occurs in northern South America from north-eastern Colombia to the Amazon delta, Cuba, Hispaniola, the Bahamas and in the Galapagos. (Roger Tory Peterson sug-

118

Greater Flamingo (*Phoenicopterus ruber roseus*)

gests, along with others, that the Galapagos population is a separate subspecies
of *P. ruber* as yet undescribed.) *P.r. roseus*
breeds in southern France (Camargue)
and southern Spain (Coto Doñaña).
Most European birds winter in East
Africa. Also breeds in parts of North and
East Africa; the Middle East and Caspian regions to western Siberia; south
through Afghanistan to Pakistan (Sind).
Occurs throughout India, but rare in
Bengal and Assam; also rare in Bangladesh. In Sri Lanka it is both resident and
nomadic, also migrates locally.

119

Family—Gruidae

Cranes
(14 species recorded)

Sarus Crane
Grus antigone

Description Standing 156 cm to top of head. A very large grey bird with long neck and legs. Head and upper neck featherless, naked skin red, pale greyish-green on crown. Elongated tertiaries whitish, drooping over grey tail. Lower neck broadly banded with white feathers immediately below red upper neck. Primaries and primary wing coverts black; underwing grey. Bill pale greenish-fawn but dark at tip. Legs and feet reddish-pink. Sexes alike but female slightly smaller. The Burmese Sarus Crane (*G.a. sharpii*) has no band of white feathers on lower neck, and plumage is darker overall.

Characteristics and Behaviour The bare red skin of head and upper neck, and pale greyish-green skin of crown are diagnostic. Takes to the wing rather laboriously but once airborne its flight is strong with powerful strokes of those broad wings. On rare occasions it is seen to soar and circle at height, but the flight is usually around tree-top level, consisting mainly of short journeys from its resting place to feeding grounds. Sarus Cranes pair for life, and the devotion and faithfulness shown by couples has become legendary in India. It is a protected species throughout its range and is very tame. *G.a. sharpii* does not enjoy the same protection and consequently is a much shyer and more wary bird.

Habitat When breeding, frequents well-irrigated plains, river beds, marshes and swamps. Often visiting close to cultivated areas during winter.

Food Diet seems to consist mainly of fish when available, frogs, crustaceans and lizards, but large succulent insects such as locusts and grasshoppers are also enjoyed. Probably less of a vegetarian than some of the other cranes, but items such as the tubers and corms of aquatic plants, green grass shoots and the like are also taken. Is well able to uproot plants to forage on their roots or search for animal matter underground.

Voice A very loud trumpeting sound, often heard as a duet between male and female, and uttered whilst in flight or on the ground. If on the ground, then both birds have necks fully up-stretched and bills pointing skywards, often with feathers fluffed out. The trumpeting serves as an alarm note, a greeting call, or merely as a means of contact between pairs.

Display Courtship display is a mutual performance, with male bird the more active partner. He will begin by half opening the wings very quickly, bowing to his mate, performing a little leap or jump; followed by dipping his foreparts up and down, then throwing his head high and trumpeting loudly. The pair then often engage in vigorous mutual bowing, followed by prancing, leaping, and a variety of other wild capers, with both birds trumpeting. The performance usually lasts for two or three minutes at a time.

Breeding The season is mainly from July to October, but may extend into December or even March. The nest is a huge collection of reeds and rushes about

Sarus Crane (*Grus antigone*)

1 m in diameter, placed on some slightly elevated position in a flooded paddy field, or on a hummock in a swamp. Two eggs are usual, these being greenish or pinkish-white, occasionally spotted and blotched with purple or brown. Average size 104.4 × 64.3 mm. Incubation period 28 days and chiefly by the female with the male standing watch. Should intruders venture close to nesting area the chicks are warned of danger by a short staccato 'kor-r-r-r', they then freeze until danger passes. Parents will on occasions try to lure intruders away using 'broken wing' tactics. *G.a. sharpii* breeds from July to September; egg size averages 102.5 × 64.9 mm.

Distribution Resident south of the Himalayas and throughout the northern parts of the Indian subcontinent, from Sind and the Punjab, eastwards through Uttar Pradesh, Bihar and northern Bengal to western Assam. Decreasing in numbers southwards. Then from Surat in the west, diagonally south-eastwards to the Godavari delta in the east. *G.a. sharpii* is resident in Assam in the Kamrup district and south to Manipur. Also breeds in Burma, Thailand, Kampuchea, Laos and Vietnam; but sparingly in the Malay Peninsula (Perlis and Perak). A rare breeding species in Australia (Cape York Peninsula).

Whooping Crane
Grus americana

Description Length 124–142 cm. North America's largest crane. Plumage predominantly white but with black tips to the wings (diagnostic) which span 2.1–2.3 m, and a deep red cap, face and throat. The red of cap and face is the skin colour which shows through the sparse black feathering. Iris yellow. Bill dark yellowish. Legs black. Sexes alike.

Habitat and Description During the breeding season frequents the prairie regions, muskeg, marshes and grassland areas. With only about 30 pairs left in the wild, the Whooping Crane is one of the world's rarest birds and a species which is in real danger of extinction. It nests in north Saskatchewan and central Mackenzie, the one to two eggs being laid in mid-May. During winter months it favours the saline coastal lagoons. The only known wintering area is the Aransas National Wildlife Refuge in Texas.

Sandhill Crane

Grus canadensis

Description Length 86–96 cm. A large, long-necked bird, standing almost 121 cm tall when fully erect. Plumage predominantly grey but with white throat and black primaries. Naked skin of cap dull red with sparse brown hair-like feathers growing at the rear. Iris orange. Bill black, relatively short and powerful. Long legs and feet black. Sexes alike. There are six races which differ slightly in plumage and size. The nominate, the Lesser Sandhill Crane, is the smallest, then there are the Canadian and Cuban subspecies (*G.c. rowani* and *G.c. nesiotes*) which are similar in size, next largest is the Florida Sandhill (*G.c. pratensis*), and the largest of all is the Greater Sandhill Crane (*G.c. tabida*).

Characteristics and Behaviour In flight it has the characteristic extended neck and trailing legs, and the distinctive crane wing beat consisting of sharp, almost jerk-like flaps. Because its eyes are positioned near the top of its head, the Sandhill Crane can look over the crest of raised ground without being seen. Its plumage affords it effective camouflage.

Habitat A bird of the wet regions on the open prairies and tundra during the summer; retiring in winter to wetlands, grasslands, grainfields and farmland.

Food Its summer diet is rather varied, ranging from roots, seeds, berries and leaves to a variety of animal food including grasshoppers, beetles, snakes, tadpoles, frogs and even young birds and eggs. During the winter it feeds on wheat, barley, flax and grasses.

Voice On the wing it has a high rolling and repeated 'gar-ooo-ooo-ooo' which has great carrying power, often heard before the bird comes into sight. It also has a repertoire of guttural 'tooks' and a goose-like 'awnk'.

Display Courtship activities include a curious dancing ceremony in which several birds walk around with heads raised before suddenly lowering them and starting to hop high in the air with raised and falling wings, increasing the speed of the display, sometimes jumping over each other and all the while uttering guttural croaks.

Breeding The nest is usually sited on the ground and sometimes standing in a few inches of water, the large flat-topped structure is composed of vegetable matter, often with a base of twigs, and can stand as high as 2 m. The two eggs are buff coloured, blotched with browns and measure 96 × 61 mm. They are laid April to June, both birds incubating for about 30 days. Some nest sites are occupied year after year. There is evidence that Sandhill Cranes pair for life.

Distribution The Lesser Sandhill Crane (*G.c. canadensis*) breeds in the Canadian and Russian arctic, in North America as far south as northern California, wintering in an area from central California east to Texas and south to Mexico. *G.c. tabida* breeds in the northern USA and less often in southern Canada. *G.c. pratensis* nests only in Florida and southern Georgia. The Mississippi Sandhill (*G.c. pulla*) has only been found in Jackson County, Mississippi. *G.c. rowani* nests in central Canada and *G.c. nesiotes* breeds in Cuba and the Isle of Pines. The Cuban, the Mississippi and the Florida subspecies are non-migratory.

Sandhill Crane (*Grus canadensis*)

Wattled Crane

Grus carunculatus
(Bugeranus carunculatus)

Description Length 119 cm. Feathers on crown dark grey. Rest of head and neck down to upper breast white. Bare facial skin red (deeper red in male) and covered with small rounded excrescences in front of the two white wattles. Mantle, breast, primaries, tail and tail coverts black. Remainder of back and wings pale grey. Elongated inner secondaries project well beyond tail. Iris deep reddish-orange. Bill pale orangey brown. Legs and feet black or dull grey.

Habitat and Distribution A bird of the open wilderness, very rarely met with close to forest regions. Sometimes frequents settlements of human habitation. Breeds in open grass and sedge marshes close to grassland meadows. The nest is a pile of compact grasses and sedges in which the one or two eggs are laid between May and August. It is a resident bird of central and south-western Ethiopia, eastern Congo, Zambia, Zimbabwe, Malawi, Botswana, Tanzania, south-western South Africa, and southern Angola, with a possibility that it also breeds in Somalia.

Common Crane

(Grey Crane)

Grus grus

Description Length 115 cm. Predominantly slate grey with black face and throat. White stripe on side of head curves downwards along length of neck. Naked skin on nape dull red. Elongated browny-grey tertiaries tipped with black and droop in a mass over tail, thereby concealing it. All flight feathers black. Iris orange-red or reddish-brown. Bill dull green, paling and becoming yellower towards tip. Legs and feet black. Sexes alike. The Eastern Common Crane (*G.g. lilfordi*) is similar to, but lighter than, nominate race.

Characteristics and Behaviour Distinguishable from storks and herons by its shorter bill and long plumes drooping over tail. Slow and graceful when walking, but very shy and wary, stretching upwards with long neck held erect whenever suspicious. Slow but strong in flight, wing tips broad and truncate, neck and legs extended. Unlike storks (which have no flight formation), Common Cranes assume either a V formation or single file.

Habitat When breeding, chooses lightly flooded boggy terrain, swampy regions and reed beds. During winter months frequents river banks, lagoons, fields and steppes, avoiding wooded areas.

Food In winter, when feeding in flocks, cultivated areas are visited and much damage is caused to newly sown fields and ripening cereal crops. Is also fond of the ground nut (*Arachis hypogean*) which it unearths in quantity. Water melon crops are also said to be damaged, the fruit being jabbed with their pointed bills. Feeding usually takes place in the evening and early morning.

Voice The loud, high-pitched trumpeting 'krook-krook' or 'kr-ooh' is uttered in a variety of keys and carries for great distances; even when the bird appears as just a dot in the sky the call can still be heard. It does have other calls such as hissing and a guttural 'kr-r-r-r'.

Display Similar to other cranes; during courtship indulges in mutual bowing, various forms of posturing, leaping, prancing and much trumpeting.

Breeding From late April to June. The nest is a very large collection of dried vegetation forming a pad and constructed on marshy ground. The two eggs are greenish-brown to greenish-olive, blotched and spotted with some shade of brown. Incubation is shared by both birds for a period of 28–30 days. Nest building and care of young are also shared.

Distribution Breeds in Scandinavia and northern Germany, then from eastern Europe and Russia to the Ural Mountains. Occurs locally in Turkey and Asia Minor. Also locally in the Danube delta, and possibly but sparingly in Spain and Yugoslavia. Most birds journey to north-eastern Africa for the winter, but others visit Iran, southern Spain, southern France, Italy, parts of Yugoslavia and Greece. *G.g. lilfordi* breeds east of the Ural Mountains, probably from the Yenisei basin to the Kolyma River in Siberia; in Inner Mongolia on Lake Tari and on the Onon and Argun Rivers. Winters in northern India, China and Hainan Island.

Common Crane display

Japanese Crane
(Manchurian Crane)

Grus japonensis

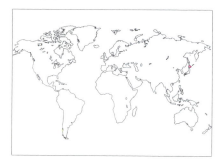

Description Length 136 cm, the largest crane in Japan. A white bird with red crown. Throat, neck and lores black. Secondaries and tertiaries long and black, drooping over the white tail. Bill greenish-brown. Legs and feet black. Sexes alike.

Characteristics and Behaviour Distinguished from the White Stork (*Ciconia ciconia*) by its red crown, shorter bill, white primaries and black legs and lores. However, it is unlikely that the two species could ever be seen together because their areas of distribution do not overlap. The white body readily distinguishes the Japanese Crane from other species of crane. In flight the neck and legs are extended, the wing beat slow. They require a run before 'take off', and adopt a V or line formation.

Habitat When breeding they frequent vast marshy areas. During winter months they can be seen foraging on cultivated land.

Food Feeds on marshland singly or with family. Diet probably includes vegetable matter, insects and small reptiles.

Voice Probably a loud trumpeting as other cranes.

Display Typical of the genus with bouts of dancing, leaping, mutual bowing and trumpeting.

Breeding A large but shallow nest composed of twigs and reeds is constructed on the ground in some swampy region. The eggs are two in number, and have a pale yellowish-brown ground, blotched with brown and spotted grey. Information concerning egg size and incubation period is lacking.

Distribution A resident species, breeding in eastern Hokkaido in Kushiro on the Kutcharo marsh, also on the Nemuro Plain. Now a protected species and it is planned to establish a Natural Park for Japanese Cranes in Kushiro, where there has been a noticeable increase in numbers: 40 birds recorded in 1953 and 200 by 1969. During winter months cranes occasionally visit the crane resort in Kagoshima, Kyushu.

Siberian White Crane

Grus leucogeranus

Description Standing 140 cm to top of head. Plumage almost entirely pure white, the long black wing tips often not being visible in a standing bird, hidden by secondary plumes. Naked skin of face reddish. Iris creamy golden yellow. Legs and feet long, may be flesh pink or rusty red. Bill, culmen to nostril dark orange-brown, remainder dusky pink becoming red towards base where it meets with naked red facial skin. Sexes alike.

Characteristics and Behaviour In flight the black wing tips become very apparent and this similarity with the White Stork (*Ciconia ciconia*) could cause confusion. Unlike other cranes, more prone to wading in shallow waters. Very wary and extremely difficult to approach, except in areas where it is protected. Usually encountered in small family parties of about three or four.

Habitat Causes very little, if any, damage to cereal crops, unlike the Demoiselle Crane (*Anthropoides virgo*) and Common Cranes (*G. grus*). Frequents swampy regions all year.

Japanese Crane (*Grus japonensis*)

Food Diet consists almost entirely of bulbs, corms and the new growth of aquatic plants. Also seeds, and an intake of coarse grit which is inevitable as the bird probes in mud, often with head submerged in the shallow water. Items are also picked from dry land.

Voice A musical and not unpleasant 'koonk-koonk', principally when in flight.

Display Assumed to be as for other members of the genus, and including prancing, leaping, mutual bowing, and much trumpeting.

Breeding Said to be similar to the Common Crane but studied very little because of the inaccessibility of its breeding terrain in remote areas of Siberia. Season about June, the nest an untidy collection of vegetable matter. Two greenish-olive to greyish-olive eggs are laid, these spotted with reddish-brown. It is thought the incubation is shared by both birds, for a period of about 28 days.

Distribution Breeds locally in southeastern Russia; in Siberia, south to Turgai; the upper Ob; northern Turkestan; Transbaikalia and Ussuriland. The vast swampy regions of the tundra rivers, and those of the forest-tundra zone, are usually snow-covered until early June. The three main breeding areas are the lower Ob, the tundra marshes between the Yana and the Indigirka Rivers; and the upper Lena. Two-thirds of the world's population (700 pairs) breeds in the region between the Yana and Alazeya Rivers. A regular winter visitor to north-western Pakistan and India, where it returns year after year to specific quarters, such as Pyagpur jheel (Uttar Pradesh), Kealadeo and Ghana, and Bharatpur (Rajasthan). Winters in China also. Birds begin to leave their wintering grounds in April through May. The world population was estimated in 1960 to be between 1000 and 1400; a revised estimation five years later suggested almost 2000.

Hooded Crane

Grus monacha

Description Length 91 cm. The 'hood' refers to the bird's white head and neck which is white for approximately three-quarters of its length. Rest of plumage dark slaty grey with long drooping plumes hanging over tail. Areas of naked red skin on forehead and lores, naked skin of forecrown also red but with black bristly feathers. Iris yellow. Bill greenish with reddish tinge towards base. Legs and feet dull reddish. Sexes alike.

Characteristics and Behaviour Very much smaller than the Sarus Crane (*G. antigone*), and distinguished from the Grey Heron (*Ardea cinerea*) by its white head, darker body plumage, and outstretched neck. The absence of black and white neck stripes prevents confusion with the Common Crane (*G. grus*). When suspicious, it stands upright with neck held erect. Nowhere is it numerous, even during migratory movements seen only in small parties. In flight the neck is outstretched and the legs extend beyond tail, a chevron or single file formation is usually adopted.

Habitat In summer frequents open plains and marshes; during winter months may be seen on marshes, in fields of rice stubble and estuaries.

Food Obtains food in typical crane fashion, by probing and picking from the surface. Diet consists principally of vegetable matter such as grass shoots, grain, tubers and shoots of cereal crops; also insects and small reptiles.

Voice A trumpeting 'kr-rooh' and a guttural 'kr-r-r-r' very similar to Common Crane, also a few hissing notes.

Display Thought to be as for other cranes, such as mutual bowing, prancing, posturing and trumpeting.

Breeding Little recorded, but probably typical of the genus.

Distribution Breeding range thought to be south-eastern Siberia from Lake Baikal to the Amur; south to north-western Mongolia and Ussuriland; also Korea and Japan. Precise information on this is lacking. Winters in China south to the Yangtze valley; in Japan restricted to Arasaki in Kagoshima Prefecture, and Kumagemachi in Yamaguchi Prefecture. Small numbers are said to winter in Manipur (India) but confirmation required.

Black-necked Crane

Grus nigricollis

Description Length 140 cm. A tall grey bird with long black neck. Crown and lores featherless, the naked skin dull red. Rest of head black with a small patch of white feathers behind eye and below it. Tail hidden by long drooping plumes of black feathers. Iris yellow. Bill either horny grey or horny green, becoming more yellowish towards tip. Legs and feet black. Sexes alike but female a little smaller.

Characteristics and Behaviour Differs from the Common Crane (*G. grus*) which has broad white band running down sides of neck, and naked red skin only on nape. Said to be a very sedentary species. Those birds wintering in the Api Tani Valley are said to be unafraid of people in tribal dress, otherwise a very shy bird. In February and March, before leaving the Api Tani Valley, the Black-necked Cranes begin to trumpet loudly whilst feeding, and engage in bouts of prancing.

Habitat During summer months inhabits lakeland regions high in the Tibetan Plateau at altitudes of 4300–4600 m. In winter frequents open fallow, paddy fields and swampy areas at altitudes of 1500 m.

Food Probably as for the Common Crane, but only record is of fallen grain.

Voice A loud trumpeting similar to, but higher in pitch than, the Sarus Crane (*G. antigone*).

Display Courtship display comprises mutual bowing, leaping, prancing and trumpeting. Very similar to the Sarus and other cranes.

Breeding The Black-necked Cranes are said to arrive on their breeding grounds towards the last week of May and leave again in October. The main breeding season being from May to July. The nest is a large mound of vegetation constructed on marshy ground, but eggs have been found laid directly on the spongy grass of treacherously boggy marshes in the Manasarowar region of western Tibet. The two eggs are olive-grey or greenish-grey in colour, faintly blotched with reddish-brown, particularly at the broad end. Size 101 × 64 mm. Both birds probably share the incubation and caring for young. Period of incubation not known.

Distribution Rare and with a very restricted distribution. Breeding occurs in the lakeland regions of high central Asia from Ladakh to Koko-nor, including the Tso Kar and Tso Moriri Lakes, at altitudes of 4600 m, also the Tibetan Plateau facies and Assam. In winter occurs from Yunnan to Tonkin. According to the local inhabitants, a flock of about 30 birds or so arrives in the Api Tani valley during November, staying in the area until late February; this winter visit of the Black-necked Cranes has taken place annually dating back to beyond living memory.

Brolga
Grus rubicunda

Description Length 105–120 cm. Head almost featherless, skin of crown olive-green, bare skin of face and nape red. A tuft of greyish feathers is present over the ears and there are fine hair-like feathers growing on its black pendulous chin. Rest of plumage predominantly silvery grey, becoming darker on the tail; flight feathers brownish-black. Iris yellow. Bill olive-green. Legs dull grey. Sexes alike but female smaller.

Habitat and Distribution Frequents grassland and cultivated areas, also the marshy borders of fresh and brackish waters. The nest is a rough platform of sticks and grasses situated on or close to moist ground. Two eggs are laid between October and April. A sedentary species except for movements between breeding and feeding grounds. Breeds in the north and north-west of Western Australia, Northern Territory except for the southern half, throughout Queensland, and into northern New South Wales. Is very common in the north, uncommon to rare in the south. Also occurs in south-east New Guinea.

White-naped Crane
Grus vipio

Description Length 119 cm. Larger and of a paler grey than the Hooded Crane (*G. monacha*) with red facial skin. Head and nape white; foreneck black. Body plumage plain grey; wing coverts dull white; tertiaries white and extremely long, projecting beyond the tail. Bill yellowish. Legs red. Sexes alike.

Habitat and Distribution Frequents cultivated fields of rice stubble, marshes and estuaries. The nest is a flat structure of dry grass situated on a slight elevation amongst the marshes of the steppes. One or two eggs are usually laid. Breeding range extends from Transbaikalia and north-western Mongolia, eastwards through Manchuria to the Amur and Ussuri Rivers. During the winter it resides in central China to the Yangtze valley in the east, south Korea and southern Kyushu in Japan, with a few birds occurring in Ussuriland.

Blue Crane

(Stanley Crane)

Anthropoides paradisea

Description Length 102 cm. Crown, nape, lores and chin slaty white; neck pearly grey above, becoming paler lower down. Remainder of plumage, including the basal neck and chest plumes, slate grey. Primaries, tips of secondaries and long inner secondaries black. Iris brown. Bill pale yellow ochre, tinged strongly with pink. Legs and feet dark grey or black. Sexes alike.

Characteristics and Behaviour A large, unmistakable blue-grey crane, usually seen in pairs and often observed soaring at great heights. As a garden pet it is in great demand, but its ferocious pecking habits make it a danger to children.

Habitat Much less of a swamp bird than the other species of crane, frequenting the short green grass of the pastured hillsides and other grassy country regions, although it invariably roosts in water.

Food Because its diet includes a high proportion of locusts it is considered highly beneficial to agriculture. A variety of other insects, worms, reptiles, fish and small mammals are also taken, as well as bulbs, seeds and other vegetable matter. Although the cranes are looked upon with favour during years of abundant locusts, they can cause damage to wheat, corn and other crops.

Voice Its call is a guttural and distinctive croak 'krraaaarrrk', very loud and repeated several times. An alarm call of 'karrooo' is also uttered and resembles the note produced when incubating birds change over.

Display Their courtship activities involve dancing rituals for periods of up to four hours duration. A pair of cranes will run around in circles, stopping to pick up beaksful of grass which they toss into the air and kick when they alight back on the ground, all the while uttering loud calls. After this the pair once more run around in small circles repeating the performance over again.

Breeding A slight raise of bare ground serves as the nest site. The actual construction varies, it can be amongst short grass and sedges growing in shallow water where no nest material is evident. At other times nest sites are chosen on grassy hillsides, again void of any actual nest structure. Those that breed amongst rushy overgrown areas build fairly substantial nests of rushes. Birds breeding on high ground construct a flat surface from small stones and tiny pebbles which are very neatly positioned. The usual clutch is two buffy-brown eggs, heavily spotted all over with various shades of brown, the shell surface being finely but visibly pitted. Size 95 × 59 mm. The breeding season is between October and March. Both birds share the incubation for a period of 29–30 days.

Distribution The Blue Crane occurs south of the Zambezi River and is confined chiefly to eastern South Africa, from the grasslands to Karoo. Has also been sighted in Mashonaland (Zimbabwe).

Blue Crane (*Anthropoides paradisea*)

130

Demoiselle Crane

Anthropoides virgo

Description Standing 76 cm to top of head. A small and principally grey crane. Head and neck black, the lower neck feathers elongated and pointed, falling over breast. Crown grey; white ear tufts grow from behind eye to form a white plume which hangs over nape. Long brownish-grey sickle-shaped plumes hang over tail. Flight feathers and tips of elongated tertiaries black. Iris varies from reddish-brown to crimson. Bill pale greenish, tipped with red. Legs and feet black. Sexes alike.

Characteristics and Behaviour The long black feathers of the lower neck extend lower over the breast than in the Common Crane (*G. grus*). Enormous flocks visit the Indian subcontinent: one such flock (mixed with Common Cranes) recorded from the Punjab, was said to extend as a broad band for about 2.5 km. The Demoiselle Crane is very difficult to approach and soon takes to the wing. In flight the neck and legs are extended. On ground it walks in an elegant manner with deliberate steps. The latter part of day is spent resting, usually on an open sandbank in a river.

Habitat When breeding it frequents low-lying marshes along rivers, and areas of scrub growth. In winter favours wheat and paddy fields; also stubble fields, and sandy river beds.

Food Its liking for grain causes damage to cereal crops on a tremendous scale. Every year, cranes in their hundreds of thousands feed on newly sown or stubble fields of wheat and paddy, as well as ripening crops (mainly when on their wintering grounds). Insects, small reptiles and amphibians are also taken. Feeding takes place during the morning and early evening.

Voice A loud 'krook-krook', higher pitched and a little softer than in the Common Crane. Also a loud trumpeting 'kr-rooh, kr-rooh'.

Display On their breeding grounds pairs of Demoiselle Cranes assemble in large gatherings to perform their elaborate communal display which includes mutual bowing, leaping and prancing with ear tufts raised and breast plumes spread. These ceremonies take place morning and evening.

Breeding Season extends from May to July. The nest is usually constructed on dry ground, on the bank of a shallow river or small islet in mid-stream. It is a simple structure of dry grasses and other vegetation. A clutch of two eggs is usual, these are green or grey but blotched with reddish-brown. Incubation period 25–30 days, female probably accepting the major role, with male bird on guard. Young are fed mainly on small reptiles, amphibians and other animal matter; a vegetable diet in winter.

Distribution Breeds south of the forest belt in the drier regions of southern Siberia, as does the Common Crane, extending westwards around the north of the Caspian and Black Seas; no longer breeds in Romania. Also breeds locally in northern Morocco and Tunisia, the Middle Atlas Mountains and Plateau of the Shotts in Algeria. May on occasions breed in southern Spain but very sporadic. Winters west of the Red Sea in eastern Africa, around the Persian Gulf, and eastwards to Pakistan and India, except the very south.

132

Demoiselle Crane (*Anthropoides virgo*)

Crowned Crane
Balearica pavonina

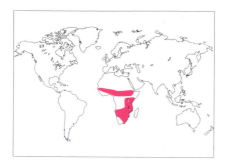

Description Length 102 cm. General plumage colour black, contrasting with the white of the upper wing coverts, the innermost of which are straw coloured. Secondaries rich chocolate brown; under wing coverts white. Head handsomely decorated, crown displaying an upright tuft of stiff straw-coloured bristles, and the white cheek patches offset by a patch of red above and below the eye and a red throat wattle. Long feathers of lower neck droop elegantly over the breast. Iris grey. Bill, legs and feet blackish. Sexes alike. The South African Crowned Crane (*B.p. regulorum*) is similar to the nominate but slightly larger and has grey instead of black on the neck and breast. Slight variations also occur in the subspecies with some birds having the white cheek patch extending more towards the crown.

Characteristics and Behaviour In flight its wing movements appear slow and almost laboured, although the bird is in fact, a strong flier. The neck is carried in a downward curve with the head positioned below the level of the body, the legs trailing behind at an angle. For the most part they are shy and wary, and not gregarious, although species of this genus are frequently tame and semidomesticated.

Habitat Essentially a bird of the open plains where it frequents the borders of rivers and swamps.

Food Feeding is not dependent on the proximity of water and they are quite at home searching areas of cultivation. Food is obtained by stamping the feet to flush any hidden prey in the form of locusts, grasshoppers and a variety of other insects. Reptiles and frogs are also taken, as are seeds and grain.

Voice On the wing it almost invariably utters a loud and ringing 'ya-how, ya-how, ya-how', with the occasional guttural grunt. During the rains it is said to have a hollow booming sound.

Display Courtship activities are spectacular, the bird indulging in a series of hops and prances with wings held outspread, often jumping 1–1.25 m off the ground, and on landing sets one foot down after the other rather elegantly. Half a dozen or so birds performing in unison is a unique sight and equal to anything seen on the ballet stage.

Breeding The nest is usually placed way out in a swamp in the midst of a well trampled down area and is a conical structure of grass, rushes and reeds; although nests in low, flat topped trees have been recorded. The clutch consists of two to three eggs which when newly laid are white and glossy, marked sparingly with purple and brown spots, soon becoming stained and dirty brown. Size 80 × 58 mm. Recorded breeding during September in Darfur; October and November in Equatoria. Incubation is shared by both sexes for about 30 days. The eggs of *B.p. regulorum* are greenish or bluish with a white overlayer, and measure 84 × 56 mm. Breeding period is between December and February, and in the Nairobi National Park, chicks have been seen during May and June.

Distribution Its range lies in Africa, being found in southern Sudan, southwestern and central Ethiopia, and rarely in the extreme north of Uganda and

South African Crowned Crane
(*Balearica pavonina regulorum*)

Kenya. It formerly bred along the White Nile to Khartoum. *B.p. regulorum* also breeds in Africa; its range extending from eastern Zaire, Uganda, Kenya, Tanzania, and north of the Pangani River to Uganda including Albert Nyanza and Lake George, south to about Port Elizabeth in South Africa, and west to Namibia. It is sometimes regarded as a separate species, *B. regulorum*. *B.p. ceciliae* breeds in Sudan and Ethiopia. *B.p. gibbericeps* eastern Zaire, Uganda, Kenya and northern Tanzania.

135

Family—Aramidae

Limpkin
Aramus guarauna

Description Length 61 cm. A large bird with an overall dark brown appearance, somewhat resembling an ibis. Upperparts dull olive-brown with a greenish metallic gloss. Head, neck and upperparts covered with numerous white flecks, becoming larger and more prominent as they extend onto the mantle and shoulders. Bill long, orange, slightly decurved and rather flat, becoming darker at the tip. Legs brown.

Habitat and Distribution Frequents marshy areas either in the open or under the cover of woodland, although it does occur in much drier areas, particularly in the Antilles. The large bulky nest, constructed of rushes and sticks, is situated on or above the ground depending on the depth of the surrounding water. Four to eight eggs are laid. Hunting has taken its toll on the Limpkin population in the past, but today it is a fully protected species. Its breeding range is confined to the tropics and subtropics of the Americas. The nominate occurs in northern South America to Paraguay and Argentina. *A.g. pictus* occurs in south-east USA, Cuba and Jamaica. *A.g. elucus* occurs in Hispaniola and Puerto Rico. *A.g. dolosus* occurs from southern Mexico to Panama.

136

Family—Eurypygidae

Sun Bittern
(1 species recorded)

Sun Bittern
Eurypyga helias

Description Length 46 cm. Head dark with white superciliary and moustachial stripes. Body plumage predominantly dark above and pale below. Wings and tail greyish brown ground but intricately patterned with numerous bars of black and white; tail displays two black bands, one at the tip, the other half way along; the middle of each wing has an area of deep reddish-orange with a paler margin. Iris deep red. Bill, upper mandible dark, lower mandible orange. Legs dark brown.

Habitat and Distribution A bird which frequents dense tropical forests, and damp marshy areas interwoven with numerous streams and rivers. The nest is usually constructed about 2–3 m above the ground, and is a bulky structure of twigs, moss and leaves. Two to three eggs are usually laid. It is the sole member of its family, breeding in one of the world's remaining unspoilt areas in eastern Peru, northern Bolivia and Brazil south of the Amazon and eastwards to 60°W; also the Guianas. *E.h. major* breeds from Tabasco and Chiapas in southern Mexico, southwards to western Colombia and western Ecuador. *E.h. meridionalis* breeds from São Luiz about 45°W curving south-westerly through about 18°S and meeting the eastern limits of *E.h. helias* and *E.h. major*, but mainly southern and central Peru.

Family—Rostratulidae

Painted Snipe
(2 species recorded)

Painted Snipe
Rostratula benghalensis

Description Length 25 cm. In breeding plumage the female is by far the more showy of the sexes. Head, nape, throat and upper breast chestnut (blackish towards lower part of breast) with a narrow band of light brown running from base of bill backwards across crown. A distinctive white rim around eyes extends backwards towards nape, giving a 'spectacle' effect. Rest of upperparts metallic olive, but separated from chestnut areas of head and breast by a wide band of white which continues from shoulders to meet up with the white underparts. Male lacks the chestnut of head and breast; upperparts olive, and olive and buff streaks. Rim around eye buffish; underparts white. Iris olive-brown to dark brown. Bill pale to dark fleshy brown; greenish at base (pinkish in female when breeding). Legs and feet yellowish to olive-green, sometimes tinged with brown or medium grey. Outside breeding season sexes are very similar and difficult to differentiate.

Characteristics and Behaviour
Has long slender snipe-like bill, with downcurved and slightly swollen tip. Skulks about in rail-like fashion, being more active in the hours from dusk through to dawn. Usually flushed singly or in groups of two or three, but most reluctant to leave the safety of dense vegetation. Flies slowly with legs left dangling for some distance before extending them horizontally to project beyond tail. Soon returns to earth when it runs swiftly through the cover of undergrowth, working its way back to the spot whence it arose.

Habitat Prefers marshy regions with pools, areas of mud and a growth of shrubby vegetation. Reed beds and lotus pools are also frequented, the thick mud of paddy fields being far less attractive to it.

Food Acquires food by probing deeply into mud, or by using a side to side movement of the bill in shallow water (in much the same manner as the spoonbills) accompanied by a bobbing movement of the hindquarters in Sandpiper fashion. Takes crustaceans, insects, worms and molluscs, also a little vegetable matter in the form of seeds or rice grains.

Voice As breeding approaches, the female produces a long 'ooooook' (much like the sound produced by blowing across the top of a bottle neck), uttered mainly from dusk and at intervals throughout the night, particularly if moonlit. The call rate is approximately one per second, lasting for a period of 20 to 80 calls before a break. During periods of daylight 'roding' at heights of 3–4 m above ground, single calls are often uttered. The male produces what is described as a squeaky note.

Display Just as with the phalaropes, the female is the dominant partner. She also takes more than one male, and can be very pugnacious as she competes with rival females for prospective suitors.

Breeding Occurs almost throughout the year but principally from July to September in India; and November to April in Sri Lanka. The nest, built by the male, is a depression in a grassy tussock, usually at the edge of a marsh, and lined with grass. A normal clutch would be four eggs (sometimes only three). These have a yellowish ground, boldly and densely blotched with shades of blackish-brown. Size 36 × 25.5 mm. After completing her clutch the female leaves the male to incubate alone (period not known), and to care for the young, whilst she finds new partners; it is thought that several clutches are produced.

Distribution Resident throughout India and Pakistan, up to about 1800 m in parts of the Himalayas. Also throughout Sri Lanka, up to about 1300 m in the hills of Uva Province. In Africa breeds south of the Sahara to Cape Province, also Madagascar, Egypt, Saudi Arabia; and southern Asia from Asia Minor through Iran to south and east China, Japan (central and southern Honshu, Shikoku and Kyushu), Burma, Malay Peninsula, Kampuchea, the Philippines, Borneo, Sumatra and Java. *R.b. australis* has a widespread distribution throughout Australia, with the exception of Cape York Peninsula and the northern parts of Northern Territory.

South American Painted Snipe

Nycticryphes semicollaris

Description Length 23–26.5 cm. Upperparts almost black, offset by two prominent buff streaks which run down the back. Wing coverts display conspicuous white oval spots. Crown has a buffish stripe; two yellow-buff bars are present on side of head. Underparts predominantly white. Iris dark brown. Bill purplish-brown. Legs and feet dark greyish-blue. Female larger.

Habitat and Distribution Inhabits areas from sea level up to 2150 m where it frequents dense marshes, deep vegetation and swampland. The nest, which is well hidden and usually placed in damp vegetation, is interwoven with grasses, reeds etc. Two white eggs are laid. Breeds in Chile from Coquimbo south to Arauco, also Rio de Janeiro and Rio Grande do Sul in Brazil, in the Paraguayan chaco, in Uruguay, and in Argentina south to Rio Negro.

Painted Snipe

Family—Haematopodidae

Oystercatchers
(10 species recorded)

Blackish Oystercatcher
Haematopus ater

Description Length 50–52.5 cm. The largest of the oystercatchers occurring along the Pacific coast of South America, and altogether different in coloration. Plumage wholly black. Iris reddish. Bill orangey red. Legs and feet pale flesh coloured.

Habitat and Distribution The vast range of this oystercatcher has equipped it with adaptive powers for varying habitats; from the calm waters of Peruvian beaches to the bleak stormy, rain-lashed, desolate coasts of places like Desolation Island and the Cape Horn archipelago. In its northerly range it shows a decided preference for rocky coasts, promontories, and offshore islets, rather than sandy beaches. One to two eggs are laid in a scrape in the bare earth or shingle. Breeding range extends from Cape Horn, northwards along the entire 4250 km of the Chilean coast, to Arica at 18°S, and continuing along the Peruvian coast up to about 7°S. On the Atlantic side it ranges from the Staten and Falkland Islands northwards, beyond the range of the Magellanic species (*H. leucopodus*) and at times reaching the shores of the Rio de la Plata in Argentina, and Uruguay.

Black Oystercatcher
Haematopus bachmani

Description Length 45.75 cm. An entirely black oystercatcher. Iris red, eye bordered by a yellow ring. Bill orangey, stout and chisel-shaped. Legs and feet orangey.

Habitat and Distribution Frequents rockbound harbours, barren reefs and rocky shores. The two to three eggs are laid in a simple depression on the shingle beach. Occurs along the Pacific coasts of North America, its breeding range extending from Alaska south to southern Baja California. *H.b. frazeri* occurs from southern Baja California to western Mexico. Resident all the year round throughout most of its breeding range, with Alaska and northern British Columbia being the exceptions.

Chatham Island Oystercatcher
Haematopus chathamensis

Description Length 48 cm. A pied oystercatcher very similar to the South Island Pied Oystercatcher (*H. finschi*). Differences include a less distinct colour demarcation line on the chest, less white displayed in wing pattern and smaller areas of white on lower back and rump. Iris red. Bill, legs and feet orangey red.

Habitat and Distribution Favours rocky coastal areas. Breeding range is confined to Chatham Island (west of New Zealand) where it is widely distributed along the coasts. A sedentary and non-migrating species.

Sooty Oystercatcher

South Island Pied Oystercatcher

Haematopus finschi

Description Length 46 cm. Head, neck, chest, upper back, wings and tail black. Lower back, characteristic wing bar and underparts vivid white. Iris red. Bill, legs and feet orangey red. Females slightly larger with longer bills.

Habitat and Distribution Frequents lake shores, and river beds of inland regions up to 910 m. The two to three eggs are laid between September and November, in a simple scrape. Breeds in New Zealand along the east and north coasts of South Island, where it is resident during the winter although some birds do migrate northwards to Auckland and Northland. Sometimes treated as a subspecies of *H. ostralegus*.

Sooty Oystercatcher

Haematopus fuliginosus
(Haematopus unicolor)

Description Length 45 cm. Plumage entirely sooty black. Iris and eyelids red. Bill red. Legs and feet pinkish. Sexes alike. *H.f. opthalmicus* is similar to the nominate but is characterised by a wider area of bare skin around the eye.

Habitat and Distribution Frequents rocky shores. No nest constructed, the two eggs being laid amongst seaweed on rocky clefts or on bare sand, between September and January. Breeds throughout Australia and Tasmania in coastal localities. *H.f. opthalmicus* breeds Cape York and Gulf Country.

Magellanic Oyster-catcher

(Fuegian Oystercatcher)

Haematopus leucopodus

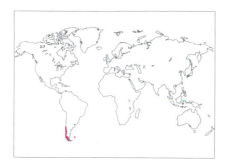

Description   Length 45 cm. Plumage brilliantly contrasting black and white. Eye offset by a diagnostic white line underneath and a yellow rim around. Bill scarlet. Legs and feet flesh coloured.

Characteristics and Behaviour Keeps company with a variety of birds such as South American geese, steamer ducks, black-necked swans and dolphin gulls.

Habitat   Frequents the coasts but also, unlike the Peruvian Oystercatcher (*H. ostralegus pitanay*), ventures great distances inland.

Food   Diet consists mainly of numerous terrestrial and intertidal invertebrates, with a possible preference for oysters and mussels.

Voice   It even excels the Magellanic Plover (*Pluvianellus socialis*) as a 'watch dog' and can be heard at any hour of the day or night with its high-pitched whistles and melodious plaintive calls.

Display   No information.

Breeding   Two dark greenish eggs are laid on the ground with no semblance of a real nest. The eggs are much darker than those of other species of oystercatcher, whether they are laid on the

Magellanic Oystercatcher (*Haematopus leucopodus*)

coast or on marshy ground inland. The background in these rainy regions is usually quite dark and lighter coloured eggs as laid by other species would prove far too conspicuous. Size 57 × 40 mm on average.

Distribution   Breeds on the Pacific coast southwards from Valdivia in Chile (where it is but a casual breeder), and regularly from Chiloé Island to Cape Horn, Tierra del Fuego and Staten Island, also in the Falkland Islands. On the Atlantic coast it moves north in winter to Chubut.

African Black Oyster-catcher

Haematopus moquini

Description   Length 42.5 cm. The dark brownish-black feathers of head and upper surface have broad dull blue-black edgings. Tail also brownish-black. Upper wing coverts similar in colour to upperparts and with brownish-black quills; inner web somewhat browner. Under wing coverts and axillaries blackish. Eye-wattle orange-red; iris ruby red. Bill orange-red. Legs and toes purplish-rose. Sexes alike. Immature birds are browner than adults and feathers from lower throat down to belly have whitish edging; iris reddish-brown; bill orange; legs and toes dark flesh colour.

Habitat and Distribution   Confined to the south-western and southern coasts of Africa from Angola south through Namibia to the Cape; from the southern Cape to Natal it is quite rare. The African Black Oystercatcher occurs in pairs or small flocks, but out of the breeding season as many as 40–50 birds may congregate together. Frequents the rocky shorelines where it feeds on mollusca and crustacea. Usual call is a piping whistle 'klee-eep, klee-eep'.

European Oyster-catcher

Haematopus ostralegus

Description Length 43 cm. Easily recognised by its bold black and white plumage. Mantle completely black, off-set against snowy white of underparts and rump. Tail white but edged with a broad black band. Iris ruby red, the eye being very prominent. Bill long, straight and bright orangey red. Legs and feet pinkish. In winter plumage it acquires a white collar which runs across the neck. Sexes alike. The Peruvian Oystercatcher (*H.o. pitanay*) is of similar size but has blackish-brown and white plumage. There is a diagnostic white line beneath the reddish eye. Bill scarlet. Legs flesh coloured.

Characteristics and Behaviour On the ground, walks and runs with a certain elegance. Flight usually strong, fast and direct, low over the shore or water and with short but regular wing beats. Outside the breeding season they are very gregarious and assemble in large flocks. Able to swim and dive when forced to do so.

Habitat Frequents rocky and shingly seashores, although in the north of Britain they may be seen inland on agricultural ground near water. *H.o. pitanay* frequents sandy beaches and sand dunes, preferring a more tranquil habitat. Does not venture inland.

Food Feeds on terrestrial and inter-tidal invertebrates, especially bivalve molluscs and limpets etc. Mussels are dragged from rock pools and prised open with the powerful bill. Crabs and other crustaceans are also taken.

Voice Has a variety of calls, the most familiar being a loud 'pic, pic, pic'. Its alarm call is a strident 'kleep, kleep'. A long piping trill, varying in volume and tempo, serves as the song.

Breeding Nesting site can vary from shingle banks, rocks and sand dunes to grassy interiors near rivers and lakes. A mere scrape serves as the nest, with little or no lining, in which a clutch of two to four eggs is laid. These are pale buffish-brown, marked with blackish spots and blotches. Average size 57 × 40 mm. Breeding season extends from May to June, both male and female sharing the incubation period of 24–27 days. It is one of the few waders that actually feed their young, a favourite item being the larvae of tipulids (craneflies); also the caterpillars of moths. *H.o. pitanay* lays two to three eggs between October and December in a scrape in the sand or shingle, sparsely lined with beach debris.

Distribution In Europe and Asia the species breeds all along the coast from the Kanin Peninsula on the Barents Sea to north-west France, including most of the Baltic coasts, Iceland, the Faroe Islands and the British Isles. In southern Europe its breeding range is discontinuous and lies along the coasts of north-west and east Spain, Portugal, southern France, northern Italy, northern Yugoslavia, northern Greece and western Turkey. Then along the west coast of the Black Sea through Bulgaria and Romania, eastwards along the northern coast of the Black Sea to the northern coast of the Caspian Sea. From there it ranges northwards across Russia, keeping west of the Ural Mountains to 55°N; south along the east coast of the Caspian Sea to 37°N; and eastwards across

European Oystercatcher (*Haematopus ostralegus*)

Siberia to about 85°E. There is a small and separate distribution in Iran south of the Caspian Sea. The nominate breeds in Europe, Asia Minor and North Africa. *H.o. pitanay* breeds from Ecuador southwards along the Pacific coast as far as Chiloé Island in Chile. South of this point it is replaced by the Magellanic species (*H. leucopodus*) and in the northern part of its range it is less in evidence than the Blackish Oystercatcher (*H. ater*). However, along the Chilean coast from Arica to Chiloé Island it is by far the most abundant oystercatcher. *H.o. pratti* breeds Bahama Islands. *H.o. galapagensis*, Galapagos Islands. *H.o. durnfordi*, east coast South America. *H.o. melacophaga*, Iceland and Faroe Islands. *H.o. occidentalis*, British Isles. *H.o. longipes*, Russia and Siberia. *H.o. osculens*, northeast Asia, China and Japan. *H.o. meadewaldoi* east Canary Islands. *H.o. longirostris*, Aru Islands, New Guinea, and Australia.

American Oystercatcher

Haematopus palliatus

Description Length 43.75 cm. A large black and white wader, and one of the shyest and wildest of all North American shorebirds. Head and upperparts black. Wings long, black and pointed with a large white characteristic patch. Underparts pure white. Iris red. Bill red. Legs and feet pinkish-red.

Habitat and Distribution Frequents broad, sandy beaches, estuaries and low, flat sand reefs. The two to three eggs are laid between March and July. Breeds along the Pacific, Atlantic and Gulf coasts of the USA, from lower California southwards on the Pacific side, and from New Jersey south to the Gulf of Mexico and Panama on the Atlantic side, including the West Indies and the Galapagos Islands. In South America it breeds southwards on the Pacific side to Chiloé Island in Chile, and on the Atlantic side to Chubut, occasionally Santa Cruz in Argentina, also Aruba, Curaçao, Bonaire, most of the Venezuelan islands, Trinidad and Tobago. Sometimes treated as a subspecies of *H. ostralegus*.

American Oystercatcher

Northern (Variable) Oystercatcher

Haematopus reischeki

Description Length 48 cm. A bird of variable plumage, some entirely black, others displaying a small amount of white on the belly. The black form is browny black and void of a purple gloss. Distinguished from the South Island Pied Oystercatcher (*H. finschi*) (when in the pied form) by its larger size, more crouched posture, the smudgy blurring of its markings and the duller white of lower back and wing bar. Iris red. Bill, legs and feet orangey red. Females a little larger and bills more pointed.

Habitat and Distribution Predominantly of the coast, where it frequents both rocky shores and sandy beaches. Rather a late nester, the three eggs being laid between December and January. Breeds on sandy estuaries on North Island, New Zealand, with the pied form greatly outnumbered by the black, particularly in the Bay of Plenty. On South Island it occurs as far south as Kaikoura and Fiordland, but again the dominant form is black. Nowhere a numerous species.

Family—Charadriidae

Plovers, Dotterels
(62 species recorded)

White-headed Plover
(White-crowned Plover)

Vanellus albiceps
(Xiphidiopterus albiceps)

Description Length 30.5 cm. Head, neck and upper back grey; crown has a longitudinal central white streak which is continuous with the white of forehead; the grey of upper back edged with black followed by white. Beneath eye conspicuous white spot; in front of eye long penduline greenish-yellow wattles. Shoulders of wings black; secondaries and inner primaries white. Mantle and scapulars brown, outer edge of the latter white. Wings display long sharp spurs. Tail white with a broad black band across the latter half of the feathers. White of chin extends in a narrow line down the throat joining the completely white underparts. Iris yellow. Legs and feet greenish-yellow. Bill yellow with black tip. Sexes alike.

Habitat and Distribution Inhabits river sandbanks following their course even into the coastal forest zone. The nest is a scrape in the sand or shingle banks close to the water's edge, lined with pebbles and small twigs. Two to four eggs are laid prior to the onset of the rains, between April and May in the north, August and October in the south of its range. Breeds in Africa from Macias Nguema and Liberia to the Sudan, northern Angola, Zambia, Tanzania, the Limpopo River and Mozambique.

Blacksmith Plover

Vanellus armatus
(Hoplopterus armatus or *Antibyx armatus)*

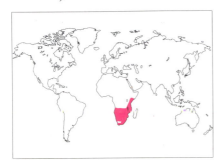

Description Length 28–30.5 cm. Being of pied appearance it bears a certain resemblence to the Long-toed Lapwing (*V. crassirostris*). Forehead, crown, hindneck, upper tail coverts, belly, under wing coverts and rump white. Upper wing coverts and scapulars light grey. Wings carry sharp spurs. Back of head, face, neck and breast blue-black. Tail white with broad black terminal band. Iris bright red. Bill, legs and feet dull black. Sexes alike.

Characteristics and Behaviour Easily distinguished from the Spur-winged Plover (*V. spinosus*) by its white, not black, crown. Usually a shy and wary bird, but becomes aggressive on its breeding and feeding grounds.

Habitat Essentially a bird of wet regions, favouring short grassy areas alongside streams and rivers, especially where flood waters dampen the surrounding flats. Also frequents areas of open grassland in the evening where it forages in the wake of grazing cattle. May be encountered on land that has recently been burnt.

Food Feeds on insects and their larvae, worms and molluscs.

Voice Normally a silent bird, becoming vocal only when its breeding or feeding territories are disturbed. At such times it will fly at the intruder uttering a harsh metallic 'klink, klink, klink', which resembles the sound of a blacksmith's hammer striking the anvil.

Display No information.

Breeding As with so many of the genus the nest is a simple hollow or scrape in the ground with a rough lining of dry grass, plant debris, and often a few small pebbles; usually not far from water. Two to four eggs are laid which closely resemble those of the Crowned Plover (*V. coronatus*), having an olive-brown ground colour, boldly blotched with black. Size 40 × 29 mm. In Kenya breeding has been recorded from April to August; and in Cape Province during September. Incubation continues for 26 days with both birds participating in this and in the rearing of the young.

Distribution Its breeding range lies in Africa and extends southwards from the Rift Valley in Kenya, and Angola, to South Africa; excluding the dry areas of Namibia.

Blacksmith Plover (*Vanellus armatus*)

148

Southern Lapwing

Vanellus chilensis

Description Length 33 cm. Fore-crown black with rear white margin. Hindcrown, back and upperparts pale copperish ashy green. Occipital crest long, thin and black. Rump white; tail black, bordered with white at base and tip. Greater wing coverts white; median wing coverts glossy metallic purplish-green; scapulars reddish-bronze but white at base and tipped with black. A long sharp red spur occurs at bend of wing. Breast and centre of throat black; belly white. Iris and eye ring red. Bill red at base and tipped black. Legs rosy flesh colour. Sexes alike. *V.c. fretensis* is smaller than the nominate.

Habitat and Distribution Frequents cultivated fields and damp meadows. Laying commences in mid-winter (July), the nest being a mere scrape in ground with a sparse lining of grass. The nominate occurs in Chile from the Copiapó Valley in Atacama, to Llanquihue and Chiloé, being especially abundant in the cultivated meadows of the central valley from the latitude of the Aconcagua River south to the lake district and Chiloé Island. Local seasonal migrations. *V.c. fretensis* replaces the nominate in Chile from the province of Aisén south to Tierra del Fuego, and in Argentina from Chubut south to Tierra del Fuego. Less abundant than the more northerly nominate, only occurring as a summer visitor in the southern end of its range. *V.c. lampronotus* occurs from southern Brazil to central Argentina, and Uruguay. *V.c. cayennensis* occurs in Colombia, Venezuela, northern Brazil and the Guianas.

150

Grey-headed Lapwing
Vanellus cinereus

Description Length 37 cm. Head
and neck entirely grey; back light
brown; rump, under wing and upper tail
coverts white. Tail white with a broad
black band. Primaries black, secondaries
white. A band of medium brown and
black separates the ashy grey neck and
breast from the white underparts. Iris
red, lappet and rim of eyelid yellow. Bill,
terminal third black, rest of bill bright
yellow. Legs and feet also bright yellow.
Sexes alike.

Characteristics and Behaviour A
gregarious species, may be met with in
flocks of up to 50 or so in number, or
small parties of six or seven birds. In
flight the black primaries, white secondaries and white underwings help with
identification. Behaviour similar to that
of the Red-wattled Lapwing (*V. indicus*),
with which it often associates.

Habitat Frequents ploughed and
stubble fields, riverbanks, and wet pas-
tureland.

Food Diet consists chiefly of insects,
but it will take worms and small crustaceans.

Voice A plaintive 'chee-it, chee-it',
also a call very like that of the Red-
wattled Lapwing but a little harsher. On
the wing a quick 'pink-pink'. If approached and caused to flush, it will
utter a call resembling 'did-all-eat'.

Display Not recorded.

Breeding Peak season seems to be
from mid-May to mid-June. The nest is
but a depression on bare open ground.
Four eggs are laid, olive-brown, spotted
and blotched with blackish, similar
in shape and colour to the Lapwing
(*V. vanellus*); size not recorded. Both
birds probably share the incubation
(period not recorded).

Distribution Breeds in Mongolia
and China south to the Yangtze Valley,
also Manchuria, Korea and Japan.
Winters in southern China, eastern
India, Burma, Malaya and Indochina.
One record from Luzon in the Philippines.

Crowned Plover
(Crowned Lapwing)

Vanellus coronatus
(Stephanibyx coronatus)

Description Length 30.5 cm. Forehead and crown black, the latter having a white coronal ring from which the bird receives its name. Remainder of upperparts buffy brown, and separated from the pure white of belly by a narrow black marginal band. Face, neck and breast buffy brown. Rump and tail white, the latter having a broad black subterminal band. Iris orange; eye rim yellow; young have biscuit-yellow iris. Bill red with black tip. Legs and feet reddish-orange; greenish-yellow when young. Sexes alike. *V.c. demissus* is similar to the nominate but has much paler underparts, chest and throat.

Characteristics and Behaviour Usually shy birds. They move about with short runs, their bodies held horizontally and heads stretched forward. Normally seen in pairs, becoming more gregarious as the breeding season comes to a close.

Habitat Frequents areas of dry open grassland, especially where grass is short or has been recently burnt. It may occur at considerable elevations.

Food Diet consists chiefly of beetles, grasshoppers and locusts, which are picked from the ground with quick thrusts of the bill. It is a bird which is highly beneficial to agriculture.

Voice Often very noisy, especially if disturbed on its breeding grounds when it utters a low scolding 'kwirk'. In flight its cry rises to a high pitched 'kree-kreeip-kree', alternating in volume. If the nest is approached the bird alights close to the intruder, and advances with outspread wings calling vigorously. Will sometimes use wing-trailing tactics.

Display They indulge in communal dances, also formation flying and aerobatics in the evening.

Breeding A simple ground scrape, usually lined with fine gravel, serves as the nest. The clutch consists of two to three eggs (sometimes four). They are buffish-brown, heavily spotted and blotched with black, and have dark grey undermarkings. Size 37 × 27 mm. The majority of egg laying occurs in the African spring months of July and October, with a less intense period during March in some areas. Incubation is shared by both sexes for a period of 28–32 days.

Distribution One of the more common members of the Charadriidae family breeding in Africa, its range extending from East Africa to Angola and South Africa. *V.c. demissus* breeds in the northern parts of Somalia and in East Africa.

Crowned Plover (*Vanellus coronatus*)

Showing the relatively large prey which the
Crowned Plover can take

Long-toed Lapwing

Vanellus crassirostris
(Hemiparra crassirostris)

Description Length 30.5 cm. Head white; rear of crown, hindneck, and upper back glossy bluey black. Remainder of upperparts, including mantle and scapulars, ashy grey, but shoulders of wings white. Throat, underside of neck, under wing coverts and belly white. The gleaming blue-black of chest and breast meets with the black of upper back. Tail and flight feathers black; wings having small knobs. Iris red; red rim around eye. Bill pink with distal third blackish. Legs and feet pinkish-grey, pink above knee joint. Sexes alike. The White-winged Plover (*V.c. leucoptera*) differs from the nominate in that all but the three outer primaries and the secondaries are white instead of black.

Characteristics and Behaviour Outside the breeding season it is a shy bird, usually seen in pairs or family parties. When alarmed prefers to run rather than take to the wing.

Habitat Essentially a bird of watered areas, mostly on floating vegetation.

Food Feeds on insects, concentrating largely on grasshoppers and beetles, and molluscs.

Voice Has a metallic alarm call of 'tip-tip' which is usually uttered in flight. The call of *V.c. leucoptera* is a loud, rather plaintive 'wheet'.

Display No information.

Breeding The nest is a well-made structure of weeds and mosses in the shape of a platform in shallow water and built up from the bottom of the swamp. Two to three eggs are laid, these vary from buff to olive-green or clay colour, boldly and fairly heavily streaked and spotted with dark browns and black. Size 44 × 30 mm. Has been recorded breeding during January and February in Uganda. Breeding season of *V.c. leucoptera* is between June and September in Malawi and between September and December in southern Zimbabwe.

Distribution Its breeding range lies in Africa and extends from Lake Chad to the southern Sudan, Tanzania and Malawi. The breeding range of *V.c. leucoptera* extends from southern Zaire and Tanzania to Mozambique and Zululand. Interbreeding between the two races occurs in Tanzania, also northern and central Malawi, hence *V.c. hybrida*.

Sociable Lapwing
(Sociable Plover)

Vanellus gregarius

Description Length 33 cm. In breeding plumage crown, back of head and broad eyestripe black. Forehead white with broad band of white extending over eye to back of neck. Sides of face creamy buff, rest of upperparts vinous grey. Throat and upper breast pale ashy grey. Lower breast blackish, shading to chestnut; abdomen and vent white. Tail white with black band. Iris brown. Bill, legs and feet black. In non-breeding plumage crown and nape brown; forehead buffish-white; a brown line extends from lores through the eye to ear coverts. Lower back white; tail white with black band. Remainder of upperparts ashy grey. Chin and throat white; breast mottled grey and brown. Rest of underparts pale ashy grey. Sexes alike.

Long-toed Lapwing (*Vanellus crassirostris*)

Characteristics and Behaviour
Diagnostic features during winter months when birds are in flight, include the distinctive dark crown and nape with broad white margin, black band across white tail, and large patch of white on wings. Before the spring migration, can be seen in flocks of between 20 and 100 birds, at other times usually met with in small parties of four or five. Mannerisms, behaviour and flight are typical of the genus and very similar to those of the Lapwing (*V. vanellus*).

Habitat Frequents ploughed and stubble fields, as well as other stretches of dry land close to cultivated areas. Far less attracted to marshes and similarly wet situations than the White-tailed Lapwing (*V. leucurus*).

Food Known to feed on grasshoppers, crickets and other such insects.

Voice A single wailing note delivered from the ground and in flight. In no way resembling the calls of the Lapwing. In winter months a very silent bird.

Display Not on record.

Breeding Occurs chiefly from mid-April to mid-June. The four pear-shaped eggs are laid in a scrape on bare ground or in grassy pasture. They are in shades of olive-brown, spotted and blotched with black or blackish-brown, very like those of the Lapwing. Both sexes share the incubation. Egg size and incubation period not recorded.

Distribution Breeds in southern and central Russia, Kirghiz Steppes, Transcaspia and western Siberia to Tomsk and Lake Zaisan. Winters from north-eastern Africa to the Sudan and northern India.

Red-wattled Lapwing

Vanellus indicus

Description Length 33 cm. Head, neck and breast black. Fleshy wattles in front of each eye crimson. Upperparts bronzy brown with a broad white band running from behind the eyes down sides of neck and merging with the white underparts. Iris sorrel to red; eyelids crimson. Bill red to reddish-orange, black at tip. Legs and feet vary between bright yellow and greenish-yellow. Sexes alike. Two subspecies: Ceylon Red-wattled Lapwing (*V.i. lankae*) is a little smaller and rather deeper coloured above, with a purplish gloss. The Burmese Red-wattled Lapwing (*V.i. atronuchalis*) has no white line on neck, but a white patch near the ear coverts. A narrow band of lilac or white separates the bronzy brown of back from the black neck.

Characteristics and Behaviour
Somewhat crepuscular or even nocturnal, spending most of the daylight hours drowsing on some mid-stream rock or the like. The flight is generally rather slow but can become very agile and swift when intercepting an intruder, or taking evasive action from a hawk. In flight look for black bands on rear edge of secondaries, black primaries, large white patch in secondaries, white upper tail coverts, white tail tip, and white wing lining.

Habitat Frequents watery situations in open country, ponds, rivers, rain puddles and ditches; also in open forest land. During the rainy season it is not uncommon to see a pair on the grassy shoulder of a highway.

Food Dusk and dawn are the principal times for feeding, but on well moonlit nights it may continue through until daybreak. Runs about very erratically in quickly changing directions, with intermittent stops when the bill is dipped forward to pick up some item of food. Ants, beetles, caterpillars, and a variety of other insects are all included in the diet; also molluscs, and a small quantity of vegetable matter.

Voice A loud and very penetrating call described as sounding like 'did-ye-do-it' or 'pity-to-do-it', which may be repeated once, twice, or several times over. Variations such as 'did-did-did-did' and 'kab-kab-kab-kab' are often produced during dive bombing tactics against intruders. Both sexes use these calls.

Display Not recorded.

Breeding The main breeding season is from March to August or September, with peak periods varying depending on locality. A mere scrape in the ground serves as the nest, lined with pellets of mud or even goat droppings, the outer margin ringed with small pebbles or pieces of dry cow manure. Sites such as fallow fields, or dry stony land are often selected. The four eggs are pear-shaped, coloured in varying shades of grey-brown, blotched and spotted with blackish-brown. During excessively hot weather the feathers of breast and abdomen are often moistened before spells of incubation, which is undertaken by both sexes (period not recorded). Egg size 42 × 30 mm. *V.i. lankae* breeding season chiefly April to August. *V.i. atronuchalis* breeding season chiefly March to April.

Distribution A resident bird making altitudinal migrations in both spring and autumn. Breeds throughout Pakistan

156

Red-wattled Lapwing (*Vanellus indicus*)

and India. Very common in Nepal Valley during rainy season, south through the peninsular India to Kanyakumari. *V.i. lankae* is resident in Sri Lanka. *V.i. atronuchalis* is resident south of the Brahmaputra River in Assam, also Manipur, Mizo, Bangladesh, Burma, southwestern Yunnan, the Malay Peninsula and Indochina. *V.i. aigneri* occurs Middle East, Iraq, south-west Iran, southern Saudi Arabia, and Afghanistan to Pakistan.

White-tailed Lapwing
Vanellus leucurus

Description Length 28 cm. Head, back of neck and upperparts pinkish-brown. Forehead and superciliaries pale greyish-white. Chin, throat and front of neck ashy grey; breast darker grey; belly pinkish-buff; under tail coverts reddish-white. Iris brown to deep red. Bill black. Legs and feet pale yellow. Sexes alike.

Characteristics and Behaviour In general appearance similar to the Yellow-wattled Lapwing (*V. malabaricus*), but lacks the black cap and is almost always seen near water. May be identified in flight by distinct black and white wing bands, and also the white on lower back and tail. On migration travels in large flocks, but on reaching its winter quarters moves around in small parties of 6 to 25 birds, when it is often seen in association with redshanks and other waders. Individuals in a flock at rest will regularly be seen to raise both wings vertically above their back, as if signalling their presence. The flight is slow and regularly incorporates a rapid fluttering of the wing tips. Gregarious at all times.

Habitat Frequents the marshy margins of lakes and swamps.

Food Included in the diet are molluscs, tiny freshwater shrimps, aquatic insects and worms.

Voice Various calls are on record, from a soft whistling note to a 'chee-viz chee-viz', or a somewhat subdued 'pi-wick pi-wick' delivered in typical lapwing fashion.

Display Not recorded.

Breeding The season extends from mid-May to mid-June. The nest is a shallow depression fashioned on the edge of a marshy area, usually in a mixed colony along with terns and pratincoles. A normal clutch would be four eggs, with both birds sharing the incubation (period not recorded but one can assume it to be as for other *Vanellus* species). Egg size 36 × 27 mm.

Distribution Breeds on the Kirghiz Steppes, also Transcaspia, parts of Syria, Iran and Iraq. Although small numbers winter in Sinai and Egypt, the main wintering grounds are in north-western India.

Javanese Wattled Lapwing
Vanellus macropterus
(Charadrius macropterus)

Description Length 28 cm. Crown, nape, face and throat glossy black. Grey collar of hindneck continues round sides of neck and over lower throat. Otherwise generally light brown above including the wing coverts, innermost secondaries and the greater coverts, but the latter are slightly paler at ends. Bastard-wing, primary coverts and quills black; secondaries pale at bases, pale ashy brown on the outer web and white on the inner web. A broad white band is formed by the base of tail and upper tail coverts, rest of tail black with a terminal band of white. Foreneck, breast and sides of body ashy brown; centre of breast and abdomen black. Thighs mainly drab brown but blackish in front. Vent, under tail coverts, under wing coverts and axillaries white. Iris brownish-black. Bill black but pale flesh colour at base, with white oblong wattle which is darkish at the point. Legs bright orange becoming yellow on tarsus; dark brown scales on tarsus and upper part of toes.

Distribution Seems confined to Java, Sumatra, and Timor.

Senegal Plover

(Lesser Black-winged Plover)

Vanellus lugubris
(Stephanibyx lugubris)

Description Length 23 cm. Forehead white; grey of head, neck and chest merges into black on the breast. Mantle, wing coverts and scapulars brownish, tinged with an oily green cast. Secondaries snow white. Underparts, including lower breast, belly and under tail coverts, white; under wing coverts a mixture of greyish-brown and white. Tail white and, except for outermost feathers, tipped with black. Iris orange-yellow. Bill black. Legs and feet dark brown.

Habitat and Distribution Favours short grassy plains, especially areas recently burnt; also attracted to ground newly cleared for cultivation. A mere depression on the ground scantily lined with grass stems serves as the nest, in which two eggs are usually laid. The breeding season varies: January and September in Uganda; April, June and July in Kenya; October and November in Malawi and South Africa. As a breeding species it occurs in West, Central and East Africa to Natal.

Yellow-wattled Lapwing

Vanellus malabaricus

Description Length 27 cm. Crown black and silky with a thin line of white around it. Chin and throat black. Bright yellow fleshy lobes of skin just above and forward of the eyes. Upperparts sandy brown; tail white with broad black terminal bar. A thin black line separates the sandy-brown breast from the white underparts. Iris silver grey or pale yellow. Bill black, but yellow or greenish-yellow at base. Legs and feet bright yellow. Sexes alike.

Characteristics and Behaviour The white wing bar on the black wings is most conspicuous when in flight. Habits similar to the Red-wattled Lapwing (*V. indicus*) but a quieter bird less given to demonstration. When in an excited condition the black crown feathers are sometimes slightly raised. More often encountered in pairs than small parties.

Habitat Less often found in wet regions or near water than the Red-wattled. Not met with on muddy shorelines. Prefers stubble and fallow fields, or barren wasteland.

Food Diet consists chiefly of insects such as grasshoppers and beetles.

Voice A long drawn out and plaintive 'ti-eee, ti-eee', also a high pitched 'twit-twit-twit-twit' quickly repeated, and mainly used if the nest or chicks are intruded upon.

Display Not on record.

Breeding Throughout most of its range in Pakistan and India the nesting season is from March or April to July; occasionally on to August in Sri Lanka. A scrape in the dry open ground of some fallow field or similar situation, serves as its nest; unlined but on occasions a border of mud pellets or very small pebbles is added. The four pear-shaped eggs have a buff or olive-buff ground, irregularly spotted and blotched with shades of dark brown and purplish grey. Size 36 × 27 mm. Both sexes share the incubation (period not recorded). Birds regularly moisten the feathers of their breast and belly prior to a spell of incubation.

Distribution Resident but given to local migratory movements away from the wetter areas during the rainy season, thereby visiting some districts only during the monsoons. Occurs from Sind in Pakistan across India to West Bengal and Bangladesh, occasionally in the Nepal Valley, and southwards to Sri Lanka.

Spot-breasted Plover
Vanellus melanocephalus

Description Length 33 cm. Forehead, crown and nape black; feathers of the nape rather long. Small reddish coloured wattle in front of the eye and a white stripe above eye. Rest of upperparts greyish-brown, tinged with an iridescent greenish cast; greater wing coverts white. Throat and front of neck black; white chest is diagnostically marked with shortish black streaks. Rest of underparts and tail white, the latter having a black subterminal band. Legs and feet pale yellow.

Habitat and Distribution A bird of the high tablelands frequenting areas of marsh and swamp. The nest is built on grassy plains and a clutch of four eggs is laid. Breeding season in Shoa, Ethiopia is August. It can be found in the highlands of northern and central Ethiopia.

Black-winged Plover
Vanellus melanopterus

Description Length 28 cm. Male: forehead white; head and neck grey; crown dark greyish-brown. Rest of upperparts brown with a bronzy cast. Secondaries white, tipped with black creating a white band across the wing. A broad black pectoral band separates the grey neck from the white belly. Tail white with a broad black subterminal band. Iris pale yellow; eyelids thin and reddish. Bill black. Legs and feet deep scarlet. The female differs in having an ashy head and neck. *V.m. minor* is similar to the nominate but smaller.

Habitat and Distribution Confined to high ground usually at an altitude of about 2100 m where it frequents open bush country. The nest is a simple scrape sparingly lined, often on newly burnt areas, in which a clutch of three eggs is laid. Breeding season in central Ethiopia is April, and in the Ethiopia–Somalia border area, June. Its general breeding range in Africa is from eastern Sudan and Ethiopia to Kenya; doubtful if it occurs in Saudi Arabia. *V.m. minor* is a bird of highland plains and grassland areas. Breeding season in Kenya from March to July, and also November to December; in Natal from August to October. Its range as a breeding species extends from Kenya to eastern South Africa.

Masked Plover
Vanellus miles

Description Length 35 cm. Very much like the Australian Spur-wing Plover (*V. novaehollandiae*) differing only in having the black of the foreparts confined to the crown and the nape. Regarded by some to be races of the same species, rather than separate species; although they have constant differences and separate distributions they do overlap and interbreed producing hybrid offspring.

Masked Plover

Habitat and Distribution Frequents swamps, estuaries and moist open grasslands. Breeding season between September and July. Occurs in Australia throughout Northern Territory and most of Queensland except the extreme south, also north, north-eastern and the south-west tip of Western Australia. This distribution overlaps with that of the Australian Spur-winged Plover in south-eastern Queensland and south-west Western Australia. *V.m. personatus* extends to New Guinea and adjacent islands.

Australian Spur-wing Plover
Vanellus novaehollandiae

Description Length 35 cm. Crown black; face white with large distinct yellow facial wattles. Hindneck black, extending as a collar to breast but does not meet. Remainder of upperparts slaty brown. Rump white; tail white with wide subterminal black bar. Flight feathers black; wings display a large spur at the bend. Sides of neck and underparts white. Iris and bill yellow. Legs pinkish-brown. Sexes alike.

Habitat and Distribution Swamps, estuaries and open grasslands are its favourite haunts. Breeding season between July and January. Occurs throughout New South Wales, eastern South Australia, and the south-east region of Northern Territory; also the south and south-east regions of Queensland and the south-west tip of Western Australia. Occurs with the Masked Plover (*V. miles*) in south-east Queensland and south-west Western Australia. A sedentary bird with seasonal and sometimes very extensive nomadic movements, resulting in the colonisation of Western Australia and New Zealand.

Andean Lapwing
Vanellus resplendens
(Ptiloscelys resplendens)

Description Length 34 cm. Overall appearance somewhat palish, with head, neck and breast being greyish in colour. Large wing patch, base of tail and belly white. Iris rose coloured. Bill yellowish. Legs and feet rose coloured. Sexes alike.

Habitat and Distribution Found only in the high Andes regions from about 4000 m upwards, where it frequents watered valleys and plateaux. Also favours the shores of rivers and lagoons, and the fields and meadows of the puna. The nest is a mere depression on dry barren slopes, but because of the cold climate it is fairly well lined with vegetation. Breeds from north-western Argentina, western Bolivia, northern Chile and Peru to the highlands of Ecuador.

Australian Spur-winged Plover

Wattled Plover
(Senegal Wattled Plover)

Vanellus senegallus
(Afribyx senegallus)

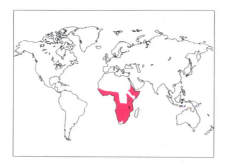

Description Length 33 cm. Male: crown black, centred with white; forehead white; neck streaked with black particularly on the sides. In front of the eye are characteristic red and yellow wattles. Remainder of upperparts olivaceous brown with white outer wing coverts. Chin and throat black, becoming a pale ashy brown on the breast, chest, and upper belly. Lower belly, under wing coverts, under tail coverts and tail white, the latter having a broad black subterminal band. Wings carry sharp spurs. Iris lemon yellow; eyelids yellow. Bill yellow with black tip. Legs and feet greenish-yellow. Female differs by having only a small amount of black on throat. *V.s. lateralis* is similar to the nominate but is easily distiguished by the area of black which divides the upper ashy brown belly from the white of the lower belly. *V.s. major* is larger than the nominate (length 34.5 cm) but otherwise similar.

Characteristics and Behaviour Usually seen in pairs or small groups. Very defensive of its breeding territory against intruders. Not a particularly shy bird and is quite often very tame.

Habitat Frequents rivers and marshes, but also favours dry open areas and cleared farmland; not too dependent on the close proximity of water. *V.s. lateralis* is particularly fond of cultivated areas and even less dependent on regions of swamp and marsh.

Food Feeds predominantly on insects and grass seeds.

Voice Has a shrill, high-pitched call of 'peep-peep' when on its breeding ground, and can frequently be heard calling at night.

Display No information.

Breeding The nest is a simple hollow on the ground with a sparse lining of pebbles and grass. Two to four eggs are laid, and these are buff in colour covered with blotches and spots of black and dark brown, average size 49 × 35 mm. Has been recorded breeding during April in Nigeria and March in southern Sudan. Incubation 30–32 days. *V.s. lateralis* breeds in August and September in Uganda, March to June in Kenya, September and October in Malawi and November in Kafue in northern Zimbabwe. Two to four eggs are laid of average size 42 × 31 mm, with Zimbabwe measurements being larger at 48 × 34 mm. *V.s. major* has been recorded as breeding from March to June in Ethiopia. Two to three eggs are laid, average size 48 × 32 mm.

Distribution Its breeding range lies in Africa extending from Senegal and Gabon to northern Zaire and southern Sudan. Breeding range of *V.s. lateralis* in Africa extends from Uganda to Angola and South Africa with only one record from Cape Province. *V.s. major* breeds in eastern Africa, in Eritrea, Ethiopia and Somalia.